1 MONT

FREE
READING

at

www.ForgottenBooks.com

By purchasing this book you are eligible for one month membership to ForgottenBooks.com, giving you unlimited access to our entire collection of over 700,000 titles via our web site and mobile apps.

To claim your free month visit: www.forgottenbooks.com/free780888

ISBN 978-1-334-94216-7
PIBN 10780888

LONDON:
SPOTTISWOODES and SHAW,
New-street-Square.

A DAY AT TIVOLI:

WITH

OTHER VERSES.

BY JOHN KENYON.

AUTHOR OF
"THE RHYMED PLEA FOR TOLERANCE,"
ETC.

LONDON:

LONGMAN, BROWN, GREEN, AND LONGMANS,
PATERNOSTER-ROW.

1849.

TO

ELIZABETH BARRETT BROWNING,

AND TO

ROBERT BROWNING,

THIS POEM,

REFERRING TO THE LAND WHICH THEY NOW INHABIT,

IS AFFECTIONATELY INSCRIBED.

386

PREFACE.

MANY of the following verses are local or occasional; and, as such, may seem to have small claim on the attention of the Public.

Still however they are published. Because the writer of even occasional verses is ever prone to persuade himself that he shall procure readers: some few, at least, who, spite of its speciality, will find it a pleasure to read what he has found it a pleasure to write.

For the chance of these few the net has been cast. And small though the draught will be, " Non ego paucis " " Offendar . . . ."

It is hardly worth while to say that some of these verses have been printed heretofore; on the ground that old things, unnoticed or forgotten, may well be allowed to pass for things new.

London, April 18. 1849.

CONTENTS.

CONTENTS.

CONTENTS.

ERRATA.

Page   3. line 2. for " yon " put " dawn's."

16. line 5. after " awhile " put comma.

29. line 14. for " Israelites " put " Exodites."

32. line 15. for " were " put " where."

76. line 6. for " her " put " his."

120. line 1. for " nets " put " net."

141. line 2. for " back " put " home."

A DAY AT TIVOLI.

ARGUMENT.

Morning. Ancient olive grove. Cascatelle. Ruined Villa. Its objects of Art, and Library. Musings therefrom. Lizards. Italian climate, and landscape, and peasants, male and female. How modified by social position. Address to Italy. Great cascade at mid-day. Italian and Swiss scenery, how differing. River Anio. Antiquarian estimate of time. Route to Italy. Ruins of Rome, and thoughts and feelings thence arising. Tivoli resumed. Italy everywhere abounding in picture, modern or ancient, or combined. Illustrated by farm house. Fountains — Vintage scene — Street Music. Reflections. A modern Roman Catholic church. Foreign travel and its proper result. After-noon-refreshment at hostel. Horace and Virgil. Mecænas and Augustus. Ruined palace of the Cæsars. Horace and Virgil resumed. Temple of Tivoli at evening. Critics. Coming on of night over Campagna.

A DAY AT TIVOLI.

PROLOGUE.

FAIR blows the breeze — depart — depart —
　　And tread with me th' Italian shore;
And feed thy soul with glorious art;
　　And drink again of classic lore.

Nor sometime shalt thou deem it wrong,
　　When not in mood too gravely wise,
At idle length to lie along,
　　And quaff a bliss from bluest skies.

B

Or, pleased more pensive joy to woo,

    At twilight eve, by ruin grey,

Muse o'er the generations, who

    Have passed, as we must pass, away.

Or mark o'er olive tree and vine

    Steep towns uphung; to win from them

Some thought of Southern Palestine;

    Some dream of old Jerusalem.

A DAY AT TIVOLI.

Come, Pilgrim-Friend! At last our sun outbreaks,
And chases, one by one, yon lingering flakes.
Come, Pilgrim-Friend! and downward let us rove
(Thy long-vow'd vow) this old Tiburtian grove.
See where, beneath, the jocund runnels play,
All cheerly brighten'd in the brightening day.
E'en in the far-off years when Flaccus wrote,
('Tis here, I ween, no pedantry to quote,)
Thus led, they gurgled thro' those orchard-bowers *,
To feed the herb — the fruitage — and the flowers.

> " Et Tiburni lucus, et uda
> Mobilibus pomaria rivis." Horat.

B 2

Come, then, and snatch Occasion; transient boon!

And sliding into Future all too soon.

That Future's self possession just as brief,

And stolen, soon as given, by Time — the Thief.

Well! if such filching knave we needs must meet,

Let us, as best we may, the Cheater cheat;

And, since the Then, the Now, will flit so fast,

Look back, and lengthen life into the Past.

That Past is here; where old Tiburtus found

Mere mountain-brow, and fenc'd with walls around;

And for his wearied Argives reared a home *,

Long ere yon seven proud hills had dream'd of Rome.

'Tis here, amid these patriarch olive trees,

Which Flaccus saw, or ancestry of these;

Oft musing, as he slowly strayed him past,

How here his quiet age should close at last.

> " Tibur, Argæo positum colono,
>   Sit meæ sedes utinam senectæ."   HORAT.

And here behold them, still !   Like ancient seers

They stand; the dwellers of a thousand years.

Deep-furrow'd, strangely crook'd, and ashy-grey,

As ghost might gleam beneath the touch of day.

All strangely perforate too ; with rounded eyes,

That ever scan the traveller as he hies :

Fit guardians of the spot they seem to be,

With centuries seen, and centuries yet to see.

Who treads this pallid grove, by moonlight pale,

Might half believe the peasant's spectre tale

Of Latian heroes old, that come to glide

Along these silent paths at even-tide ;

Or Sibyl, wan with ghastly prophecy,

From her near fane, as whilom, wandering by.

But Morning, now, and sunny vines are here,

From tree to tree gay-gadding without fear ;

Or else in verdant rope their fibres string,

As if to tempt the little Loves to swing;

Or, tricking silvery head and wrinkled stem

With tendril-curl, or leafy diadem;

A sportive war of graceful contrast wage,

The Grave and Gay—green Youth and hoary Age.

Hence we may feel Resounding Anio's shock,

As his full river thunders from his rock.

Yet mark! meanwhile adown its own small dell

How falls or winds each little cascatelle.

With no rude sound — with no impetuous rush;

But blandly—fondly—or by bank or bush.

Or floats in air; as when mild mermaid frees

(Or so they feign) her tresses to the breeze;

And careless, for a while, of coral bower,

Basks on the sunny sands till noontide's scorching
        hour.

A DAY AT TIVOLI.

How sweet! to have such gentle waters near;
Just soothing, ne'er disturbing eye nor ear.
Nor deem I those unblest, whom choice — or fate —
Leads to prefer the Lesser to the Great.

" Repose, thou better privilege than fame."—
So felt, we know, the great historic name,
Mecænas; he who owned those villa-halls,
All stately once, tho' now but rifted walls.
And hither, wisely truant, oft would come,
Forth from the smokes, the toils, the strifes of
        Rome. *
For, tho' defaced, discolour'd, broken, bow'd,
Yet were they then of gold and ivory proud.
Or far beyond what proudest wealth might do,
From thoughtful art a nobler triumph drew.

   *   " Fumum et opes strepitumque Romæ."   HORAT.

There, dark-hued urns, with mythic picture fraught,

Time's treasures! stood, from old Etruria brought;

Which even then had claim'd uncounted date,

When yon great Rome was yet a struggling state.

Or marble vases there, in white array,

Beam'd back an added lustre to the day.

Or, better, when the gladly-welcom'd guest

Came to the banquet, rich with every zest,

From lamp of chisell'd bronze, adjusted light

Threw out some Phidian marvel on the night;

Evoking, heightening thus, in form or face,

Each subtler beauty or diviner grace.

Nor yet, when hours of feast had found their
        close,

Or jaded statesman sighed for short repose,

Was wanting, there, some well-befitting room,

Nor all-too bright, nor quite subdued to gloom,

Whose odoriferous cedar-shelves along
Fair scrolls were ranged; philosophy or song.
There, all our Lost might be.   All Livy told,
(Where now?) and all Menander limned of old,
Fresh from the life; with sweet Simonides;
And glorious Sappho, — greater yet than These.

And then, perchance, yon small and sinuous rill,
In open day now glittering down the hill,
Slid underground its tube-directed path,
To feed or sculptured fount or perfumed bath.

Their graceful rites, their gorgeous prides are gone;
Their proudest monument a crumbled stone!
Yet if the marble and the bronze decay,
Their storied memories fade not thus away;
But cluster still, tho' dying centuries toll,
Beadrolls for thought, and relics for the soul.

Hence here have bowed, thro' farthest tracts of time,

Genius and Lore, from every cultured clime.

And hence, no less, thro' many a countless year,

Like us, shall unborn pilgrims worship here.

And how may pilgrim stand on spot like this,

Nor feel what flitting wayfarer he is?

Here, where the joys, the griefs, the hopes, the fears,

The busy doings of three thousand years,

Since first Tiburtus made these hills his hold,

Have dreamed their dream, and mingle with the
        mould.

Men pass like cloud, or wave, or morning dew:

A thought nor very deep, nor very new.

Yet who, as here, shall find him, face to face,

In presence of that Mighty Commonplace,

And not imbibe the moral of the spot,

Accept the general doom — and murmur not?

Yet, if All die, there are who die not All;

(So Flaccus hoped), and half escape the pall.*

The Sacred Few! whom love of glory binds,

" That last infirmity of noble minds,

" To scorn delights, and live laborious days,"†

And win thro' lofty toil undying praise.

What if for These, now verging to the tomb,

As yet, nor laurels spread nor myrtles bloom ;

Proud mortgagees they stand of Fame's estate,

And for the brave reversion bear to wait.

Nay, what tho' never from th' ungrateful soil

Green chaplets spring, for guerdon of the toil ;

In calm content their avarice sublime

May well forego those unpaid debts of Time ;

Who, e'en while clutching at the generous pelf,

Priz'd ever, most, the virtue for itself.

----

    *   "Non omnis moriar, multaque pars mei
         Vitabit Libitinam."   HORAT.

  † LYCIDAS.

So go we musing on.   But, as we go,

Just glimpse yon lizard frisking to and fro.

Now here—now there—now straightly fixed he lies ;

Then turns him sudden in a mock surprise.

Give him this southern wall, this sprightly sun,

And Past and Future are to him as One.

Tell him of either, (for he loves to talk

With loiterer, pausing on his easy walk,)

Tell him of either, and, with eyes that glisten,

And head aslant, awhile he seems to listen,

Then jerks him merry off, as if to say,

" Good Sirs ! for me sufficient is the day."

So, should grave memories ever come to press

Life's present hour with thought of past distress ;

Or future years o'erhang us, vague or dim,

Why, we may come and take a hint from him.

And who not thus delights him, who or what,

In such a clime or animate or not ?

These hill-side vines ; this wide expanding plain ;

These fields — of pasture, here ; and there, of grain ;

These twisted chesnuts, with their cheery green ;

Yon darker cypress, spired above them seen ;

Which, many a century, land-mark, there, hath stood,

Self-lifted obelisk, immortal wood ;

Those aloes, that with sworded panoply

Still warn the pilgrim, who would dare too nigh ;

Yon steeply climbing town ; that rocky height ;

Seem they not living in the living light ?

For each grey flake hath faded from the view,

And all around is one Ausonian Blue.

Not the fresh dawn, not evening's tenderest hour,

Speak to the spirit with a deeper power.

As eye and heart strain up that azure air,

What light — what love — what fixedness is there !

Transient — we *know* — Eternal — let it *seem !*

With such blue sky we only ask to dream.

E'en he, (behold ! him in that shaggy coat) —

Yon goat-herd, with his only browsing goat,

On the hill-slope ; beside that humming stream ;

This heaven above ; how can he help but dream !

He ne'er was train'd in thronging city vast,

For some huge deck to shape the mighty mast ;

To face, in ship, the deadly Afran breeze ;

Or drop the anchor deep in Arctic seas,

Like our stern sons.   Yet not for this despise,

Albeit in seeming vacancy he lies.

Not idle they the most, who idlest seem ;

Nor lost are all the hours in which we dream.

In trade's dim workshops all unused to moil,

Small share is his of luxuries won by toil.

But luxuries he hath not unrefin'd,

That please, perchance, yet more his southern mind.

Mere idlesse pleases; as supine he lies,

And gazing upward thro' the blazing skies,

Wins shifting colours to his dazzl'd eyes;

Or red or azure. And delights to see

The brilliant mockeries as they come and flee;

And wonders, why? Or makes of each a gem,

Such as might grace a pontiff's diadem;

Ruby or sapphire. Strange to me — or you;

But, here, All love this dreamy " Nought-to-do."

  Or by tradition's tongue, or ruin old,

Of his own land's great deeds hath he been told;

And asks himself, erewhile, with wishful pain,

Why may not those brave days return again?

And tho' still mingling in confusion quaint

Profane and Sacred; Warrior and Saint;

Yet each in turn hath taught him, if need were,

Like This, to suffer — or, like That, to dare.

Think too that These were they, whose flags, unfurl'd
Beneath Rome's eagle crest, once shook the world.

Yon peasant-girl, — you mark'd her where she stood,
In her just pride of conscious womanhood —
(Against yon column now she leans awhile,
Graceful, you'll own, as milkmaid by a stile.)
Behold her in her country's old costume;
Is lady statelier in a palace room?
Too poor, we know; perchance, too inly great,
The town's last mode to wish to imitate.
Barefooted — but with no submissive mien;
In beauty's regal right — a lawful queen.
Such type to Michael's chisel had given a law;
And Raphael's self but painted what he saw.

In region, where not oft the Dryad charms
Town-loving Signor to his woods and farms;

And palaces, within proud city shut,

But rarely neighbour on the peasant's hut;

(He'pr i vileg'd — or doom'd — by lot of birth

To see, but seldom, these the Lords of earth;)

'Mid equals rear'd, what other should he be

But equal too — a freeman 'mid the free?

Our nobler civil rights to him unknown,

Yet all his social freedom — all his own.

But where wealth's stringent or out-doling hand

From point to point wide stretches o'er a land;

In power or bounty ever seen or felt,

Like lictor's fasces or an almsman's belt;

Tho' order hence, with all its blessings, flow, —

As fertilizing waters guided go —

Yet as, henceforth, we lose the stream that
        played

Thro' its own runnels, free and not afraid;

C

So there, by wealth or purchased or controlled,

Word — gesture — look — in native frankness bold —

Are quelled, like sprite, beneath the Wand of· Gold.

Again — (prolix beyond the thing I ought,

You kindly bear, and let me speak my thought)

In land — where from the plough men rushed to
     arms,

Just saved a state, and then re-sought their farms —

I love these breathings free ; these heads erect ;

I love, in look and speech, this brave neglect.

With ancient memories they better suit

Than balanced phrases or observance mute.

Nay, for a spot like this seem least unmeet,

As in high natures Grand and Simple greet.

Is this the race down-dwindled to a weed ?

A rotted trunk ? or but a buried seed ?

Which, if the storm should rise and floods up-tear

The shrouding soil, and give it back to air,

Shall sprout again; .no longer matter brute;

But gladden'd with green leaves and its own glorious
       fruit.

   Oh Italy! if fallen (as some delight

To say thou art), yet fallen from what vast height;

Oh Italy! thou land of memories dear,

Yet not for these alone we prize thee here;

But gladly take thee, with acceptive heart,

Not for thy " hast been," but for what thou art.

For who that knows thy seas of brightest wave,

Their shelving shores or rocky steeps that lave;

Thy lakes, 'mid mountains laid, in soft blue length,

Like Beauty guarded at the feet of Strength;

Thy landscape, seen at morn or evening hour,

Town — village — cresting chapel — arch or tower;

Rich art—rich nature—each on each that press,

Till the sense aches with very loveliness;

Thy corn with fruitage mixed; thy realms of vine,

For ever beauteous—if they droop, or twine;

Thy balmiest clime, which daily tasks can leaven

With bliss, from out the common air of heaven;

Man's natural bearing; woman's easy grace;

From very rags—in gesture and in face;

Thy dark-eyed childhood's ever-ready smile

Of playful innocence or playful wile;

Or knows thy human nature's better part,

Swift thought, swift feeling, and the kindly heart;

And knows, beside, what thousand pulses beat

To win thy glories back, with generous heat;

Who but for thee must fervent vows forecast,

And hope thy Future, while he dreams thy Past?

But now 'tis Mid-day! and the deep retreat

Of Anio's grot must shield us from the heat.

'Twas in such deep recess Salvator's touch
Won its dark truth, and Gaspar fed on such.

Lo! the rapt river along its channel'd ledge
Precipitous hurrying to that dizzy edge.
Now, for one breathless moment, high uphung,
Like curled sea-wave ; then—forth, as foamy, flung.
Here—in long lance-like flakes—straight down; while,
      there —
As if were all uncoiled Medusa's hair,
The serpent-waters twirl and hiss in air.
Or else, in black and rocky cauldron bound,
For ever eddy round and round and round ;
Wakening the thought, or sadden'd or sublime,
Of endless toil, or never-ending time.

All types from clashing waters—all are here ;
All types and all emotions ; sound and fear ;

Pent agonies, that struggle for relief;

Free gushing tears; dishevelled locks of grief;

Mad angers; sullen pause; re-bursting ire;

With flood still swifter than pursuing fire.*

Yet beauty too.   But such as poets shed

Round   the   great   vision   of   that   snake-tress'd
         head,

Perplexing beauty — beauty wreathed with dread.

'Tis a great scene !   Yet, not by it opprest,

We feel its greatness in a buoyant breast.

For (not as when some wild Helvetian flood

Dives down its sombre depth of piny wood)

Here, all around, hath Gladness flung her braid

Of green festoons, and scattered light and shade.

*   " Sonitumque metumque,
    Miscebant operi, flammisque sequacibus iras."
                        VIRGIL, *Æneid.*

Or rather—if the word were fitlier won—
Not shade, but shadow—playmate of the sun.
Gloom glorified ! as suits a southern clime ;
And (bear the phrase) a Cheerfuller Sublime.

E'en far within the grot Light sports with Dark ;
Here—a long arrowy streak ; and there—a spark.
If disappearing, soon to re-illume ;
Like festive fire-fly, glancing thro' the gloom ;
Or old Venetian masquer, richly dight,
Who, 'neath his waxen torches' orange light,
With gems and spangles glitters on the night.

Who, Anio ! that hath come, or soon or late,
To this thy shrine, but deems the day—a date ;
Whence to recal at will, his whole life's length,
Thy voice — thy speed — thy beauty and thy
    strength ?

Whether thou tinklest from some mountain-crest,—

Thy birth-place—where the eagle builds his nest;

Or cruel bandit plants him; thence to strain

His greedy vision o'er the cowering plain ;

Or whether, wandered from thy native hills,

(As strong and stronger grown from clustering rills)

Thou pausest for a while in silent lake,

Where that she-wolf her passing thirst might slake,

Who (prowled to Tiber down and destined thus)

Suckled great Rome in infant Romulus ;

Or holdest on by feudal tower, or hall

From Cæsars named, or nameless ruined wall ;

Or by quaint villa ; such as after days

For Este's princely line made pride to raise ;

Where, many a time, thy rushing wave would roll

Intenser power o'er Ariosto's soul ;

Brightening, thro' secret sympathies, the lay,

Which here he loved to weave (or so they say);

And which for aye—like thee—shall flow along

As wild—as smooth—as playful and as strong;

Whether thou speak of simple Sabine farms,

Or call, as now, to song—or art—or arms;

Be welcome every dream thou waftest down,

And every tale; but most of old renown.

Tell us of statesman—warrior—bard—or sage—

Wonder or love of many a famous age—

What time, by seas shut in and rocky strand *,

And all-undreaming of the Roman brand,

Our Britain lay, a yet unhistoried land.

Hail and Farewell!   Resounding Anio!

And now, Fair Stream! with milder current flow

On 'mid thy vines and pasture; till thou come

'Neath the proud walls of twice Imperial Rome.

---

*   "Et penitus toto divisos orbe Britannos."

VIRG. *Ecl.*

Thence, with old Tiber, soon to sport thee free
'Mid the blue waters of the Tyrrhene sea.

Thou, Pilgrim-Friend! (we know) wert never one,
Mere idle praiser of the days foregone * ;
Nor striving still to shroud with poor pretence
Of classic feeling gap of week-day sense ;
But ever, in thy wisdom, taking heed
That worthy life is made of daily deed.
And tho' (by shrewd Saint Stephen stolen, of late,
From converse of thy friends — to serve the state)
It thee befits to pay thy studious vow
To Hansard rather than to Livy — now ;
Yet hence, methinks, 'tis joyance doubly sweet
In this, the dream-land of our youth to meet ;
Together turn again the classic page,
And win us back our boyhood's loftier age ;

* "Laudator temporis acti."   HORAT.

And church and state for some brief weeks eschew ;
And make again this Ancient World our New.

But, here, far back the scroll must be unroll'd ;
Here, where ten centuries do not make the Old.
Where old they deem in antiquarian thought
Some work by Ancus or by Tarquin wrought.
That tunnel huge, or prison Mammertine ;
Or old may grant the Fabian — Julian — line ;
But half a Modern make our Constantine ;
And, as they pass his structures, on their way,
Scarce note them — as but things of yesterday.

Small matter !   Old or new, we'll list the
    while,
As Ciceroni teach us — or beguile.
And, if some tales for question seem to call,
In sifting Niebuhr's spite, accept them all.

Where Curtius leapt, believe the very spot;
Or muse with Numa in th' Egerian grot.

　Yea—sweet for him, by parent doomed to court—
Unwilling suitor—ancient law-report;
Awhile to snatch him from the hated thrall
Of pleader's desk, or point-contesting hall;
And sweet, not less, for thee, who legislate,
To 'scape committee-room and dull debate;
Corn question—currency—and funded debt;
French marriage—and the treaty of Utretcht;
And leaving—not too long—our own dear land,
To hail—as we of late—the Belgic strand;
Thence, o'er their ill-laid rail, right glad to roll, —
Tho' shaken sore—to this Ausonian Goal.

　Not stately Bruges might detain us, now,
Nor Meuse, soft-gliding 'neath her fortress'd brow;

More pleased some while to thrust from off the scene

Battles and sieges, Marlborough and Eugene.

Nay, prizing thee, old Legendary Rhine!

Less for thy legends than thy climbing vine.

Nor yet in famed Helvetia tarrying long,

Tho' there green vales and glittering mountains throng;

And We aye pleased to feel the bosom swell,

By Uris rock, at thought of William Tell.

But onward still our purposed way we take

O'er tall Gothard and by Locarno's lake;

Or climbing slow, or if in full career,

With Rome! Rome! Rome! in heart and eye and
    ear.*

Still thirsting; till at last we came to stand,

Glad Israelites! in it — our Promised Land.

        " Roma auribus hæsit,
Roma oculis."   *Incert.*

And what our Pisgah view?   Crushed piles of
    state
The walls within ; and dun and desolate
Campagna round ; with bridge and tower destruct
By age or war; and ruined aqueduct
Athwart the fading twilight.   And is this
A Forum ? or a vast Necropolis ?
Temples — for tombs ; a nation's dust beneath ;
With silence round, that fears almost to breathe ;
And city-solitude, so strangely drear,
The Living seem to have no business — here.

If in some vineyard ground our step be stayed,
Awhile, beside the peasant's delving spade ;
(Now — vineyard; once — Patrician's client court,
When that near Forum was a world's resort)
As up and up the rank black mould is cast,
The very earth seems odorous of the Past.

Each after each, behold in turn out-thrown
Tile — faded stucco — scrap of sculptured stone.
Anon — some shattered urn, or broken frieze;
Power — turned to skeleton!   His fragments — These.

Ruins and fragments!   Is it these that Ye
From your own thriving land come forth to see?

We   answer,   " Yea ;"   these   are   the   things   that   We
From our own thriving land come forth to see.

We come to see how ancient power may die,
And ponder on a realm's mortality.
Yet, seeing how survive the Good — the Just;
In goodness and in justice learn to trust.
We come, as in fond youth, to sympathize,
Thro' backward ages, with the Great and Wise;

And feel—as then—some throb thro' inner heart,

Where life's low interests claim no smallest part.

We come from restless plan and restless deed,

Ambition's instrument, or habit's need,

To find the Calm which generous leisures give,

And less in act than meditation live.

We come from wit's and jest's enlivening strife,

And all the dearer bliss of household life,

To feed on pensive thoughts; yet not the less

To win a pleasure from our pensiveness.

And if those grave and pensive thoughts (and
    such

Our case may be) should press the heart too much;

'Twere not so very far to find our way

Mid glorious art, that tells of no decay.

Were beams each high conception just the same

As when from Grecian chisel first it came.

Tho' mortal-born, of beauty that might mate
With archetype celestial increate.
Nay, beauteous more than in their glittering prime,
Tinged softly by the sun-set hues of Time.

Then, if some friend should come, with best intent,
To warn of hours all uselessly misspent ;
He too may learn (nor is the lore abstruse)
That uselessness, like this, is noblest use.
That while the busy serfs of wealth and power
Fawn only on the Present's sordid hour,
(No lofty thought or back—or forward—cast)
We pluck our nobler Present from the Past.
Nor pause we there, but, starting forth anew,
From thence shape out a nobler Future too.

This long discourse hath led us far away
'Mid other themes from our Tiburtian day,

D

But now again, with renovated grace,

We bow before the Genius of the Place,

Full of the scene around ; and all-intent,

As slow we travel up this steep ascent,

To win the passing pictures, as they rise

From present hour, or ancient memories.

For here, glance where eye may, or footstep fall,

Or new or old, 'tis picture—picture—All.

This structure near, mere peasant's dwelling-
     place,

Is not itself without some claim of grace.

Its terraced roof, square tower, and arching gate

To Art, long since, thro' picture consecrate.

For Creed of Art hath not alone to do

With reason'd faith, but with tradition' too ;

And Beauty's self we hold for most divine,

When Memory stands Priestess at her shrine.

Behold! its sunward wall.   How all-ablaze
With one full glow of ripest, yellowest maize;
Whose rich-ribbed cylinders, in order strung,
Seem tassels, for some festal rite uphung.
Or each might be fit cresting ornament
For regal canopy, or warrior-tent.
No brighter hues hath Ceres in her horn;
No cheerier ever broke from saffron morn.
More golden — ne'er from furnace-fires were rolled
Than these, sun-wrought in vegetable gold.
Which almost might requite his absent ray,
Themselves a sun-shine for each clouded day.
While yon ripe gourds, that strew the court-yard
         floor,
Beam upward, each a mass of glittering ore.

But now, with these our rural splendours done,
And we, like them, full-saturate with sun;

How fresh it is, as, step by step, we mount,

To watch the gushings of that marble fount.

Its cistern — some antique sarcophagus;

(Here, Old and New for ever mingle — thus)

While its raised cup, whenceforth the Naiads toss

O'erbrimming wave, is fringed with greenest
      moss.

(For, in these lands comes oft from mere neglect,

What art long while might ponder to effect.)

Each pendent tuft, with sparkling spray bedript,

Seems it not emerald, with diamond tipt?

And then those female forms, with braided hair,

And heads erect, that classic urns up-bear;

(From forth whose shapely rims dewed vine-leaves
      drop; —

Thrust partly in, escaping lymph to stop.)

These, as around the cistern's edge they throng,

Say, might not These to Grecian Art belong?

Whoe'er from life's mere prose awhile would flee,

Should roam with us this land of reverie.

Where museful fancy needeth not the aid

Of cloister dim, or silent colonnade,

Or solitary shore, or moonlight glen,

But meets her visions 'mid the haunts of men;

And feels in broadest sun-light round her stream

From every waking fact some answering dream.

And how that lofty Past exalts the Now!

That churl—a Cincinnatus at the plough!

Yon kite, slow circling up the Blue—afar—

An augury! or be it peace or war.

Those very geese, out clamouring, one and all,

The Sacred Birds that saved the Capitol!

And lo! thro' yonder arch those oxen twain;

On slowly swaying that grape-loaded wain.

Right goodly creatures, beautiful to view!

Dark-hoofed—dark-maned—the rest of creamy hue;

With large soft eyes.   All soft as Here's were,

('Tis Homer's simile, so we may dare)—

When their pride slept, and love alone was there.

Now, thro' the spacious court behold they go;

Now, pause beside the pillared portico.

With foliage drest, and that rich ruby freight,

Nay—draw they not, in sacrificial state,

A Bacchic offering to some temple's gate?

Mark the · broad wheels—but two!   That yoking
          bar,

Just as of old!   No wain—but ancient car!

And they, above the piled up grapes who ride,

Their naked limbs with purpling vintage dyed,

The Fauns!   And here, ere long, the rest shall be:

Look with poetic eyes and thou shalt see

Bacchante lithe; and jesting Satyr near;

With broad Silenus, staggering in the rear,

Tho' doubly propped; while gay goat-footed Pan

'Mid pipe and cymbal triumphs in the van.

Then that old Crone, with lifted tambourine,

Which still she smites; and some strange rhythm be-
tween,

Or, rather, mixed; while to the double sound

A dark-tress'd girl is dancing round and round,

That Crone, with hair unkempt, yet scarce uncouth,

(So well it suits) and that fore-thrusting tooth,

Keen — almost prescient — tooth of prophetess;

(A flitting fancy, which I may not press)

That Crone shall be our Sibyl! And that Girl,

Still hurried round and round in dizzier whirl;

With her wild eye almost to frenzy fired,

(Such look in Delphi had been held inspired)

And flashing locks, and every flashing limb,

She shall be Priestess! and that Song—the Hymn!

And wherefore, " No?" Why may not this be
    chaunt

From Pythian tripod or Dodona's haunt?

For, as some stream, by ancient fragments hid,

From earthquake—flung; or mighty hill—down slid;

(That cumber, many a league, the valleys round

With huge grey rock or grass-grown earthy mound;)

Still holds its silent way 'neath all that hides,

Then at some far-off point once more outglides,

Another stream; another, yet the same;

E'en those, who quaff, may guess not whence it came;

No otherwise this mystic rhythm may flow,

Far winding on, from ages long ago;

Some Grecian chaunt, its secret course unknown,

And heard, at last, in region not its own.

Old customs die not, but sprout forth again;
The names distorted, while the things remain.
Fane, " Church " baptized, sees new-named votaries vow,
And old Chief Augur is Prime Pontiff, now.
E'en Jove himself, Great Jove Capitoline,
Rules in strange semblance o'er a later shrine.
His twice-fused bronze transformed, by pious feint,
From Pagan Deity to Christian Saint.

At this you smile; and who would smile refuse?
But when the smile is o'er, 'twere well to muse.

Olympian Zeus, upon his golden throne;
Calm Pallas, glorious in her Parthenon;
Or rudest Sibyl, from her rocky cave,
Mid spiky aloes, issued forth to rave;
Or curling smokes, o'er Judah wont to rise
From bull or goat, in barbarous sacrifice;

These, for rank falsehoods, while the most eschew,

In stern contempt for Gentile and for Jew;

These, for imperfect truths, let us accept;

Instalments of the universal debt;

Acknowledgment, we know, far off and dim;

Yet, not the less, acknowledgment of Him,

" In every age, in every clime adored;

(So sang the bard,) Jehovah — Jove — or Lord."

This preachment o'er, (which yet you mildly
          bear,

Of preachments all-impatient as you are),

Yon church, whence now intones the holy mass,

If so you please, we'll enter as we pass.

For churches here (with reverence be it said)

Are not too holy held for week-day tread.

But each, at will and unrebuked for wrong,

May come and muse their column'd aisles along:

And some high influence win, or grave delight

From picture, incense, or the chaunted rite;

Or find fit hour, as every passing day

Its joy or sorrow brings — to praise or pray.

But now with festal silks the shafts are bound,

And glittering fringes edge the arches round.

Of granites red, or cippolino grey,

Or carvings quaint, small sight for us — to-day.

We quarrel not.   There are, we know, who hate,

Or half unchristian deem such pious fête.

Yet silvered Saints, and Virgin fancy-drest

For peasant-worshipper may be the best.

Rare entrance his, or none, thro' palace gate;

Be this his palace hall — his room of state.

Or let him bring his humble sorrows here,

Secure, at least, of one Great Listener's ear.

These types, so falsified, from earliest youth

Have been to him the very types of truth ;

And his own toil hath helped the monthly dole

That gilds the shrine, and bids the organ roll.

Worships—like tastes— have each their power and
        tone ;

Church ne'er was meant for Dilletant' alone.

And Christians, such as would all rites confine

To their own forms, are Christians none of mine.

Then spare him, Critic ! as he kneels in this

His ill-drest fane, and loves for God's—and his.

" Of all the ills unhappy mortals know,

A life of wandering is the greatest woe." *

So thought Ulysses ; but we think not so.

And blest it is, with pilgrim-staff in hand,

At our own will to roam each ancient land,

* POPE's Odyssey, b. xv. l. 364.

(Of which in school-boy volume first we read,

Yet never dared to hope our feet should tread)

And test with manhood's sense the dreams of
     youth,

Nor lose the vision, and yet win the truth.

If nature-led; to track with pleasant pains

Their mountain-wilds and cultivated plains.

If student; in some shy monastic crypt,

To try old text by new found manuscript.

If vowed to art; its each attempt explore,

From primal Ægypt, or the Xanthian shore,

To where in Greece it triumphed; deified

And deifying; then like mortal died.

In this bright land again to spring to life,

And strive again; scarce conquered in the strife.

But he who to the land, that sent him forth,

Brings back but this, brings product little worth.

Huge virtuoso—true! But driveller blind

Beside the larger soul—the deeper mind—

Which, learning man, hath learnt to love mankind.

Our hostel hold us now ; not undistrest

By pleasant toil ; for pleasures must have rest.

Here, sit—or sleep—or scrawl the pane—your fill ;

Or rhyme—like me, (against Minerva's will!)

Who for sublimer flight nor bold nor strong,

May just achieve to journalize in song.

Yet for brief space.   For now, it seems, we dine :

Lo ! here, wild boar—and, here, Falernian wine ;

With figs—ripe grapes—and rarest wheaten bread.

And who may tell but here the board was spread

For genial Flaccus and for Maro—thus—

Two thousand years ago, as now for us ?

Just fancy ! when they sat, as here we sit,

The frolic—and the wisdom—and the wit.

And here came he, the blood of ancient kings *,

To find the joyance equal converse brings.

With them gay chatting, as the whim might be,

Of one's arch Phillis, one's sweet Lalage.

Or last year's visit to Bandusia's fount ;

Or journey planned to yon Soractes' mount.

Or laughing back, with still-recurring glee,

Those sparkling days from Rome to Brindisi.

Here too the Cæsar might consort with them ; —

His Purple laid aside and Diadem —

Well-pleased, amid their talk and easy cheer,

To glimpse his own great Rome—yet feel it not too near.

What glimpse (had glimpse been given) of years to come !

The conquering Goth ; and that twice pillaged Rome.

---

* "Mecænas atavis edite regibus." HORAT.

Gone! eagles — banners — lances — lictors' rods;

The temples crumbling o'er their crumbled Gods.

All steadfast as they seemed, his ancient stock

Uprooted from their Capitolian rock.

The far-off realms, they swayed but with the sword,

Crouched at a swordless pontiff's slightest word.

Their mighty palace (of each glory reft,

Nor marble frieze, nor porphyry pillar left;

Nor floor, as once, with rich mosaic spread;

Nor hues cerulean arching overhead)

Roofless and void; and only, now, renowned

As larger ruin 'mid the ruins round.

The baths with rubbish choked; the fountains dry;

The green acanthus, as in mockery,

(And wild, as when by chance in wicker sown,

It gave, of old, its graceful hint to stone)

Wandering, at will, amid those very halls,

Where once 'twas carved for golden capitals.

Some lingering terrace but a loftier spot,

Whence to discern that his own Rome was not.

Thee, Flaccus! the self-promised not to die,

A kindlier star hath sped thy prophecy.

Or song itself fulfils its own desire;

Realms fade away, and dynasties expire;

Yet on from age to age sounds thine—with Maro's lyre.

But here, by rightful and peculiar lot,

Ye hover most, the Genii of the spot.

Of memory—vision—feeling—thought—a part;

Heard from each lip, or borne in every heart.

Brave bliss! What braver may to bard belong?

Save its own joy from self-requiting song.

Diverse the strains. Yet would we figure how

Together oft ye trod this favorite brow.

Not now in jocund converse, as of late,

But each his inner theme to meditate.

Thou, it might be, some polished lyric verse;

Now, fondly dallying; now, brightly terse.

Or precept, each with its own wisdom rife,

That models — here — a poem; there — a life.

Or else wouldst hie thee to the busy street,

To sketch some silly pride or grave conceit.

Then round to us the playful picture turn,

And bid us in that glass ourselves re-learn.

.Meanwhile (so dream we on) the Mantuan
        Bard

To yon tall peak hath paced the silent sward.

Thenceforth to scan, in prospect calm and free,

The various plain, from hill to circling sea.

Pale region, now; with culture ill be-sped;

Then, one wide Georgic, bright beneath him spread.

Or, not unprompted by **that far sea-line,**
Would ponder o'er th' Æneian tale divine ;
Till clear before him, and in perfect plan,
The   Heroic   Vision   stood — " Arms   and   the
    Man."

    Once   more   I   move   you   (our   third   flask   is
    done,
And lo ! the shadows lengthen in the sun)
To view yon time-hued fane, at this soft hour,
When eye and spirit best may feel its power.

    Laud we the Gods !   No connoisseur is near,
With his clipp'd talk our frank delight to sear.
Who, while a thousand admirations crave,
Still harps and harps on arch and architrave ;
And, vowed to his five orders, fain would school
Our kindling spirits with his three-foot rule.

Scarce more, if we might choose our time and
    place,
Here would we wish that nobler critic race,
Æsthetical; who stand on tiptoe still,
And see far less with eyesight than with will.
Would-be discoverers, on vague voyage bent;
Interpreters " of meanings never meant; "
Of the true creed, but whose ecstatic faith
O'erpasseth ever what the Gospel saith;
These, while the smaller critics tease or vex,
With their dim dreams disturb us—or perplex;
Or, if such comment sound not civil quite,
Daze out our clearness with their too much light.

Digressive thus, ere passing thoughts be gone,
I crave your leave, and idly ramble on,
(You still indulging) till I bring you near
Our famous temple—and behold it!—here.

Amid these varying tales of ruin old, —
Some, scantly gathered up; some, falsely told —
Sibyl's or Vesta's we may hardly tell:
But he, who first devised, devised it well,
Here, where it stands, with circling columns bound,
And placed—how calm! above the gulf profound,
To tame these rugged rocks—this torrent's stress—
With power of Beauty and of Gentleness.

So might we feign, some fair high-lineaged
    queen
Rules o'er a raging crowd with look serene.
So too, when some great Master hath designed
To paint in human form th' Eternal Mind;
And humbly dares essay that lofty brow,
Which holds the Past—the Future—and the Now;
Awhile we pause before his art severe;
Then, reverent bend; yet less in love than fear.

But when, ere long, around those awful brows

In graceful curve his cherub-group he throws;

Each with its little arms — beneath — above —

Outstretch'd to clasp, and childhood's look of love;

Behold! those awful brows no longer lower,

But Sense of Love hath soothed the Sense of Power.

So — Pilgrim-Friend! our pleasant day is sped:

* "To-morrow, to fresh woods;" to-night, to bed.

Yet from these heights throw one more glance abroad,

And some few moments dream with dreamy Claude.

Beneath — are field and stream and lake and wood,

And site, where ancient city stands — or stood.

Around — the hills.   That — here — in bay recede,

As if for nestling culture taking heed;

Or boldly — there — indent the level plain,

Like promontory pronged into the main.

* LYCIDAS.

As parts for other clime th' unwilling day,

See ! how that far Campagna sinks away.

A sea of purpled land, now, seems to be ;

Now, scarce distinguished from the purple sea.

E'en while we gaze, how vanish on the view

Each bright — each fair — each fading — faded—hue!

A pensive light, while aught of light remains ;

Then — pensive veil for these Deserted Plains !

1848.

A DAY AT TIVOLI.

EPILOGUE.

FAREWELL, Romantic Tivoli!
　　With all thy pleasant out-door time;
For now, again, we cross the sea,
　　To house us in our northern clime.

Since Love and Duty both advise
　　No longer, even here, to roam;
Nor all too slackly hold the ties,
　　That cluster round the heart of home.

And bid us find old feelings there;

    And our own native pleasures woo;

Nor muse, as now, (how sweet soe'er

    The musing be) — but plan — and do.

And yet, in many an interval,

    How oft, Beloved Tivoli!

Shall Fancy hear thy waters fall;

    And Memory come — to dream with Thee.

OCCASIONAL VERSES.

UPPER AUSTRIA.

UPPER AUSTRIA.

We loved that Upper Austrian land;
    And who, that knows, would love it less?
Which, as it seems, alike the hand
    Of God and man conspire to bless.
His stream-dispensing hills, that tower,
Man's happy, lowly, household bower,
On sunny slope, in quiet dell,
These well may win a fond farewell.

How may we e'er forget the power
Of those huge hills, at sunset hour?

Peak and black ridge upheaved on high
Athwart the gorgeous evening sky,
While brightest waves beneath were rolled
In amethyst or living gold.
Or how the beams that loved to wake
With morning touch Gemunden's lake;
Or that pale moon which paused to light
Dark Traunstein's solitary height?

Nor more, Fair Land! may we forget
Thy Happy with thy Lovely met.
Those rural dwellings snug and warm,
And strong to meet the winter storm.
With casement green, and vine around;
Each in its plot of garden ground.
The most—beneath.   But some that creep
Where the sun beckons up the steep;
Near neighbours to the beechen grove,
Which mingles with the pines above.

And every little mountain-plain,
Of herb profuse or waving grain;
Where all that eye beholds is rife
With signs of well-contented life.

O Liberty! thou sacred name!
  Whate'er reproach may thee befall,
From judgment just or spiteful blame,
  To thee I cling—on thee I call.
  And, yet, thou **art** not All in All;
And, e'en where thou art worshipp'd less,
  In spite of check, in spite of thrall,
Content may spring, and happiness.

And tho', man's rightful claim to cheer,
Thy fuller beams be wanting here;
Yet happy they, if right I spell,
The folk within this land who dwell.

F

Here no hard look, no dogged eye,

Meets, to repel, the passer by;

But observation loves to scan

Mild greetings sped from man to man;

Bland courtesies; kind words that fall

From each to each, and all to all.

And here is woman's bending grace,

That bends reply; and answering face,

With servile smile not falsely deckt,

But honest smile from self-respect.

While peasant boy, with curly pate,

And arm surcharged with book and slate,

Gives frank reciprocating look,

The fruit—I ween — of slate and book.

Nor lack there signs to speak a sense

Imbibed of holier influence.

For if there be or nook or spot
  More lovely than the rest;
Beside the brook, beneath the grot,
  Some chapel neat is drest;
Whenceforth the Virgin-Mother seen,
In azure robe depict' or green,
From that her ever-blessed face
Sheds softer beauty o'er the place.
Or He, who died on holy-rood,
Is there, with thoughts of deeper mood
To sanctify the solitude.

'Tis true—for me their accents rung
In fact, as name, a stranger-tongue.
A cloud, if words alone could speak,
Thro' which no ray of thought might break.
But soul of ready sympathy
Finds semaphore in silent eye.

And smiles that play from silent lips
Clear what were else the heart's eclipse.

And One was with me, who could spell
   Whate'er each tongue might say,
And oft, I ween, their sense would tell
   In better phrase than they.
And all that German land was known
To him, familiar as his own.
Their states, their dynasties he knew,
Their folk, how many or how few;
Each tale of conquest, battle, siege,
Right, custom, tenure, privilege,
With all that appertaineth; down
From Cæsar or from King to Clown;
And all that priest or jurist saith
Of modes of law or modes of faith.

And he had comment, full and clear,

The fruit of many a travelled year;

But more, by meditation brought

From inner depths of silent thought;

Or fresh from fountain, never dry,

Of undisturbed humanity.

When first among these hills we came,

　　The Autumn lingered bright;

But winter now begins to claim

　　His old ancestral right.

He speaks intelligible speech

In the red yellow of the beech;

And mingles with the breeze a touch

Of polar air; in sooth not much;

• But such as serves to hint the day,

When he shall rule, not far away.

Fall'n leaves are straggling down the brook,

With something of prophetic look ;

Whose little eddies circle round

With more, methinks, than summer sound.

While the strong rivers, now more strong,

With dimmer current sweep along.

And frequent gust and chilling rain,

That meet the traveller on the plain,

Are telling tale of wintry war

Amid the topmost peaks — afar.

Scarce longer, Hills of whitening brow !

　　Man's summer day endures ;

And snowy flakes are falling, now,

　　On other heads than yours ;

And colder, dimmer currents roll

From Time or Chance to chill the soul.

Our fervent youth's adventurous blood

　　Defies or place or clime,

And dares the mountain or the flood,
   Thro' winter's stormiest time.
When sober eld, grown weak or wise,
Seeks gentler scenes and milder skies.

So we will seek a milder sky,
   By where slow roads up creep
Atween the summits, cresting high,
   Of some huge Alpine steep;
By easier way thenceforth to glide
Adown the smooth Italian side.

With choice before us, shall we go
   Where Stelvio winds his road,
Above the realms of thawless snow,
To where green things refuse to grow,
   Primeval frosts' abode?

Then — beating cloud, and bitter wind,
And torrent fierce left all behind —
Drop down to Como's southern bowers,
And drink the breath of orange flowers?
Or else, in idle boat reclined,
Hang loitering round that little bay,
Where erst inquiring Pliny lay
　　Thro' long observant hours;
Or haply nursed some inner dream,
Beside his intermitting stream?

Or rather shall we follow, now,
　　The waters as they roll
From rugged Brenner's lowlier brow
　　Adown the steep Tyrol;
To where Catullus loved to wake
His sweetest harp on Garda's lake?

Rich is the land, (all own its power,)
    The land for which we part,
Italia!—rich in every dower
    Of nature and of art.
And rich in precious memories—more—
From fragrant urns of classic lore.
But whether 'mid Etrurian bowers,
Where gallery spreads and palace towers;
Or where, beneath cerulean day,
Bright Naples clasps her double bay;
Or where steep-fallen Anio roves,
All peaceful now, thro' Tibur's groves;
On thee, contentment's happy home,
    Land of bright stream and hill!
Fair Austrian land! where'er we roam,
    Our hearts shall ponder still.

TO H. M. W.

ON READING HER POEMS.

BLEST is the bard, whose modest pride,
  Unlured by vapour gleams of wit,
Still clings to nature as a guide
  With following feet, that fear to quit.

And blest are they, who o'er life's road,
  Too often treacherous or abrupt,
Tho' guile betray and malice goad,
  Move kindly on and uncorrupt.

But doubly blessèd is thy part,
  Who, 'mid bad taste—bad world—still true,
Preserv'st simplicity of heart,
  As woman, and as poet, too.

SONNET

WRITTEN AFTER HAVING READ A. F. RIO'S PETITE CHOUAUNERIE.

CALL not our Bretons backward.   What if rude
Of speech and mien, and rude of fashion—drest;
Yet dwells firm faith beneath each simple vest;
With valiant heart, that scorns all servitude,
But to the Right.   When France's fickler blood
Crouch'd to the crownëd pageant of the day,
New-fangled homage These disdained to pay;
But kept old vows in truth and hardihood.
And with no surface-glare, no facet-light,
But the rich inward lustre of the gem,
When tried in shade, were yet more deeply bright.
And therefore, Traveller! call not backward—Them,
Found never yet, in worst extremity,
Backward to bear—nor backward when to die.

INSCRIPTION FOR AN EAGLE'S FOOT,

BROUGHT TO ENGLAND BY SIR CHARLES FELLOWS, AND NOW
PART OF THE FURNITURE OF HIS LIBRARY TABLE.

ME — Lycia nursed amid her blaze of day ;
Ere long, on strengthening plume I winged my way
To every peak around her mountain coast,
But o'er Phœnicus loved to hover most ;
And watch, at eve, the ever-burning flame,
That from her storied summit quivering came.
Or stooped to scan, amid the valleys lone,
Once famous cities, now but fabling stone.
At last to earth down circling, all too nigh,
Chimæra's birth place, Cragus, saw me die. —
What here remains was borne, on British prow,
By Xanthian Pilgrim — home.   I serve him now.

GROWING OLD.

AFTER THOMAS CAREW — 1630.

SHYEST Lady!—say not so;
  Say not you are growing old.
'Tis a tale that, well you know,
  Fits me most if truly told.
Then, shy Lady! be more bold—
Say not you are growing old.

Bloomy faces, surface graces,
  Pretty prattle, yea or nay;
Smiles all empty, meant to tempt ye,
  These indeed may fade away.
But the smiles that beam from sense;
But the eyes' intelligence;
But the voice with feeling fraught;
But the word of serious thought;

With self-judgment ever lowly;
These be charms that fade but slowly.

In yonder new-found world,.they say,
When summer-suns have passed away,
And autumn-cloud and fog and rain
And wind and cold are come again;
'Mid all this tristful weather-strife
Doth a new summer start to life.
Their Indian summer call they this,
And calm (they say) and bright it is.
More calmly bright, more sweetly gay,
Than that which late hath passed away.

Lady, thou hast felt the touch
Of sickness and of sorrow much;
But they now shall both be past,
Like that singing autumn-blast,

Which yet singeth augury

Of good season, soon to be.

Brighter suns shall rise before thee,

Softer breezes shall flit o'er thee.

Thou shalt have thine Indian summer;

And we will welcome the New Comer.

"NEC VIXIT MALÈ QUI NATUS MORIENSQUE FEFELLIT."

HORAT.

THEY choose not ill their lot who choose

    All quietly to live and die,

By Science sheltered or the Muse,

    In unpretending privacy.

Proud epitaph—the world's acclaim—

    These ask thou not; if, in their room,

Some few but love thy living name,

    And household tears bedew the tomb.

TO AN ÆOLIAN HARP.

Oh! breezy harp! that, with thy fond complaining,
   Hast held my willing ear this whole night long;
Mourning, as one might deem, that pale moon's waning;
   Sole listener, oft, of thy melodious song;

Sweet harp! if hushed awhile that tuneful sorrow,
   Which may not flow unintermitted still,
A lover's prayer one strain, less sad, might borrow
   Of all thou pourest at thine own sweet will;

Now when, her forehead in the moonlight beaming,
   Yon dark-tress'd maid, beneath the softening hour,
As fain to lose no touch of thy sad streaming,
   Leans to the night from forth her latticed bower;

And this low whispering air, and thy lorn ditty

    Around her heart their mingled spell have wove;

Now cease awhile that lay, which plains for pity,

    To wake thy bolder song that tells of love.

LOVE'S AUCTION.

COULD pretty Jane be put to sale,

    I'd have no auctioneer in vogue;

Not Christie should her charms detail,

    But Truth should dress the catalogue.

Within the leaves no falsehood slid;

    No grace hitch'd in which Jane hath not.

Then all the world would come and bid;

    But only Love should buy the lot.

G

RUFUS'S TREE.

O'ER the New Forest's heath-hills bare,
  Down steep ravine, by shaggy wood,
A pilgrim wandered; questing where
  The relic-tree of Rufus stood.

Whence, in our England's day of old,
  Rushing on retribution's wing,
The arrow — so tradition told —
  Glanced to the heart of tyrant-king.

Some monument he found, which spoke
  What erst had happen'd on the spot;
But, for that old avenging oak,
  Decayed long since, he found it not.

Yet aye, where tyrants grind a land,
 Let trees, like this, be found to grow;
And never may a Tyrrel's hand
 Be lacking there—to twang the bow!

FRAGMENT.

CROTCHETS—odd mixings up of soul and sense—
(Sense, if the truth were told, oft mastering Soul)
Full sure he had; but we did suffer them,
For they were gentle and obeyed the rein.
Nay—wayward fantasies, that come and go
From nerve or brain, and link and cling together
At their own will (and surely such were his)
'Twere hard, methinks, to blame!

SECOND LOVE.

The ne'er-forgetting ! him who loves but once !
Romance may laud, but Cupid dubs for dunce ;
And jeers, and mocks him on from pain to pain.
Who but hath sworn him ne'er to love again,
Then forged, himself, new links and chafed at his own
      chain ?

There are who drink, intoxicate to be ;
And some because intoxicate already.
E'en like these last, I snatched the cup from thee,
And hurried to my lip with hand unsteady.
A draught it was, from whence fond hopes, at first,
Bead round the heart, and then, like bubbles, burst.

But tho' I knew the treachery of the cup,

Thou wert the Hebe, and I drained it up.

And now, as all repentingly I lie,

Like some slow-sobering quaffer—wonder why.

IN A PORTRAIT GALLERY.

In vain, Bright Girl! you bid us mark

    Each charm of portrait round us thrown,

When sight and soul alike are dark

    To every face—except your own.

And while yon connoisseurs eschew

    All " Perfect "—save in the " Ideal;"

To prove them false we turn to you,

    And find our " Perfect"—in the "Real."

SAPPHO.

Two graceful portals led to Sappho's bower;
Two fitly graceful portals.   By the one,
A winning group, the Syren Senses stood,
Chanting their sweet temptation; while the other
Was fondly guarded by the Muses nine.
Love chose, for so it seemed, the wiselier part,
And prayed the gentle Muses.   But, no sooner,
In bland compliance with that prudent prayer,
Were the valves opened, than those wayward Senses
Fled their own gate, and thrust them in with him;
Proud of the freak—a gay, tumultuous throng.
Then first He found that 'twas delusion—All;—
Must such delusions hold him evermore?—
Those separate groups—his own fantastic dream;
And that the double gates—in sooth—were One.

LA PIQUANTE.

Quoth Flavilla, " Think I can't
Why they will call me ' piquant.' "

Yet, Flavilla! should we try,
We might find the reason why.
Be thy mien " devout and pure,
" Sober, steadfast, and demure; "
Yet—if something in thy smile
Contradict it all the while,
Is'nt this, Flavilla !—grant—
Is'nt this to be piquant?

Be thy talk not gay o'er much;
Yet—if serious-seeming touch

Stirreth ever more the string
Of some fond imagining,
Is'nt this, Flavilla!—grant—
Is'nt this to be piquant?

If when deeplier we would look
Into that half-open book,
Thou dost close it, Slyest Saint!
More to tempt us by restraint;
Is'nt this, Flavilla!—grant—
Is'nt this to be piquant?

Would we know what else may serve
This—thy mantle of reserve—
Whether thou dost shroud in it
Loving thoughts, for lady fit,
Or but some provoking wit—

If, with pretty, wilful dealing,

Now — close veiled — now part revealing —

Thou, like some coquettish nun,

Mockest still our fancies on ;

Then, just as we had hoped to win

Way the parlour-nook within,

Coolly turning, bidd'st us wait·

Thy pleasure at the outer grate ;

Isn't this, Flavilla ! — grant —

Isn't this to be piquant ?

APPARITIONS.

If, as they say, the Dead erewhile return,

Sent or permitted, from their shadowy bourn ;

Yet not, or so we trust, shall every ghost,

In his old guise, reclaim our mortal coast.

Let Spurio, if once more among us thrown,

Come back in any shape — except his own.

While, Phyllis! you, the frank and debonnair, —

Do you return — the very thing you were.

THE GREEK WIFE.

THE GREEK WIFE.

I LOVE thee best, Old Ocean! when
   Thy waters flow all-ripplingly;
And quiet lake, in inland glen,
   Might seem, well nigh, a type of thee;
And when long-lingering lights of eve
Float o'er thy waves that hardly heave.

And anchor'd vessels seen afar,
   Athwart the bay, with slanting shroud,
And crossing line of rope and spar,
   Hang pictured on the yellow cloud;
While Silence, from the placid shore,
May count each pulse of distant oar.

And Spirit-Airs—for so they seem—
　Are whispering of some far-off land.
For then doth Fancy love to dream
　Along thy visionary strand;
And winneth tender thoughts from thee,—
Perchance too tender, Gentle Sea!

No mother-home is world of our's
　For dreamy tenderness alone,
But a rude school; and sturdier powers
　That shrink not from the shock—the groan—
And hearts heroical and free
Are thy stern teaching, Stormy Sea!

Hence—from this shore we love to view,
　Yet with no meanly-safe delight,
Yon chafing surge of inky hue,
　Whose foams, all ominously white,

As the white shroudings of the grave,
Curl o'er the black and greedy wave.

And now, beneath this darken'd sky,
   By lightning flashes shown more dark,
Watch silently, with eager eye,
   All wildly tost that Grecian bark,
Whose stoutest hand scarce holds the helm
'Mid whirling waves that rush to whelm.

That bark to guide a torch's light
   Is gleaming thro' the troubled air.
Who lifts it there?   In pale affright
   A wife — a mother — lifts it there,
For him; who, spite of coming wreck,
All calmly treads his splitting deck.

And yet one pang he scarce may brook:
   He knows who lights that dangerous strand.

Oh! might he gather one last look!
   But clasp once more that loving hand!
Cease, raging Demons of the Dark!
And spare the light, and spare the bark.

She too, might power, like wishes, fly,
   Would fly to tread that deck with him.
Again she lifts the torch on high;
   But, half extinct, the torch is dim;
Or flickers useless light behind,
Back-driven by the cruel wind.

If that brave bark may triumph yet,
   No guardian Spirit comes to tell;
Or if the Fates, in conclave met,
   Hang brooding now o'er yonder swell,
As when on that disastrous night
Abydos saw the failing light.

If that brave bark may triumph yet,
   We know not how 'tis doomed above;
But this for lesson sure is set,
   That Courage firm and faithful Love,
Or if they live, or if they die,
Have each fulfilled their mission high.

Where faithful Love, where Courage glows,
   The patriot virtues take their birth,
And thrive in home's serene repose;
   Till bursting from the household hearth,
Throughout a land her every son,
At duty's call, up-starts as one.

Through what a dreary tract of time,
   Hast thou not seen, Ægean Wave!
Each dweller of thy storied clime
   A struggler, now — and, now, a slave.

H

In war, in peace, struck down, or vext,
By Roman, first; by Moslem, next.

Yet Love hath never fled thy shore;
  And Courage old still lingers there.
And them may Freedom more and more
  Still nourish, with her new-born air,
In hearts of women and of men,
Till Salamis revive again.

THE RENEWAL.

I KNEW her, when my youthful time
   Beyond the verge of manhood stood ;
And she was in her glorious prime
   Of freshly ripened womanhood.

And when her darkly radiant eye,
   With longest lash of silken jet,
Glanced forth a double witchery,
   Where sympathies and sense were met.

And o'er her rich embrownëd skin,
   All richly brown as tropic rind,
The colour mantled from within.
   As blushes told her secret mind.

And voice, and smile, and whitest gleam
　　Of forehead high thro' raven hair
Awakened in each heart some dream,
　　Which, once awakened, lingered there.

Mine lingered long.　Till, on a day,
　　I met her once again, to find
If Time may something take away,
　　He yet hath more to leave behind.

For hers was still that darkest eye,
　　And longest lash, and gleaming brow;
And smiles that won, in day gone by,
　　Were waiting still — to win us now.

And still that voice was hers; and grace,
　　Which more than youthliest bloom can thrall;
And sense, outspeaking from the face;
　　And goodness, beaming over all.

And if ecstatic hope now stirs

    Less warmly, than in hour of youth,

Some airy visions still are hers,

    'Mid many a lesson taught by truth.

And if, perchance, some hues be fled,

    If eye or smile be radiant less ;

Serener charm they own, instead,

    And win new power from pensiveness.

'Tis thus, when hearts are swept along

    Beneath some master minstrel's play,

The sweetest part of all the song

    Is where the music dies away.

But is the Music past and gone ?

    Nay, listen ! for it wakes again ;

A lay prolonged, of tenderer tone ;

    A sweeter joy from softer strain.

And therefore do I prize the day
  I met her once again to find,
If Time may something take away,
  He yet hath more to leave behind.

FLOWERS FROM WATERLOO.

WE sprang on no ignoble soil;
  'Twas on the field of Waterloo.
Our culture was the battle-toil,
  And many a hero's blood—our dew.

Yet, fair as other plants that breathe
  Their peaceful sweets we flourish, now.
Oh! where to find a fitter wreath
  For patriot's or for soldier's brow.

LINES

SUGGESTED BY ODE XXIX. BOOK I. OF HORACE.

TO

ANTONIO PANIZZI, ESQ.

AS THE WORTHY OCCASION,

AND TO

THE REV. CHRISTOPHER ERLE,

AS THE PROMPT THROWER-OUT

OF THE QUOTATION WHENCE IT HAS SPRUNG,

THIS MERE TRIFLE IS INSCRIBED.

LINES

SUGGESTED BY ODE XXIX. BOOK I. OF HORACE.

AND so, dear Hicks! on " Nature's wealth "
Your new-found phrase — and rustic health
   Intent, and cottage-life ;
You scheme from town to steal away,
And chain yourself, or so they say,
   To that grave joy — a wife.

What parish girl shall find employ
To deck the bride ? what louting boy
   Lead out the one-horse chair,
When, just at noon-day, forth you ride,
Correctly spousal, side by side,
   And sadly take the air ?

CARMEN XXIX. LIBER I. HORAT.

ICCI, beatis nunc Arabum invides

Gazis, et acrem militiam paras

   Non ante devictis Sabææ

      Regibus, horribilique Medo

Nectis catenas?   Quæ tibi virginum,

Sponso necato, barbara serviet?

   Puer quis ex aulâ capillis

      Ad cyathum statuetur unctis,

And can it be, dear Hicks! that you
For such dull raptures would eschew
 The life we lead in town?
No, Hicks! I'd just as soon believe
One might hold water in a sieve,
 Or make up-Thames run down,

As you desert the volumes rare
Panizzi buys up every where,
 Or gets by hooks and crooks;
Or bear to lose your daily walk
To the Museum, and his talk,
 Still better than his books.

Doctus sagittas tendere Sericas

Arcu paterno?   Quis neget arduis

   Pronos relabi posse rivos

      Montibus, et Tiberim reverti ;

Cum tu coëmtos undique nobiles

Libros Panætî, Socraticam et domum,

   Mutare loricis Iberis,

      Pollicitus meliora, tendis ?

LINES SENT TO ELIA,

AFTER READING HIS ESSAY ON ROAST PIG, WITH A TRIBUTARY
BASKET.

ELIA! thro' irony of hearts the mender,

May this pig prove like thine own pathos — tender.

Bear of thy sageness, in its sage, the zest ;

And quaintly crackle, like thy crackling jest.

And — dry without — rich inly — as thy wit,

Be worthy thee — as thou art worthy it.

PS.

Beside the sty-born finding room to spare,

Begs kind acceptance of himself — a hare.

And since, being sylvan, he but ill indites,

Hopes he may eat much better than he writes.

THE GODS OF GREECE.

PARAPHRASED FROM SCHILLER.

YE Gods of Greece! Bright Fictions! when
  Ye ruled, of old, a happier race,
And mildly bound rejoicing men
  In bonds of Beauty and of Grace;
When worship was a service light,
  And duty but an easy bliss,
And white-hued fanes lit every height;
  Then—what a sparkling world was this.

Creation, then but newly born,
  Felt all the glowing trust of youth;
And pulses, yet, were all unworn,
  And poesy was very truth;

And Gods were spread thro' earth and air,
　　And looked or spoke, in sight or sound;
And who but loved to worship there,
　　Where they were mingling all around?

Not then was yonder radiant sun
　　Mere globe of fire, as now they say;
But Phœbus urged his chariot on,
　　A guiding God!—and made the day.
Each hoary hill, each thymy mount,
　　Some fond presiding Oread tended;
And Naiads bent by every fount
　　From which a gushing stream descended.

'Twas Daphne's voice—so taught the creed—
　　That murmur'd from yon laurel tree;
'Twas Syrinx from the hollow reed
　　Out-sighed her plaintive melody.

No bird sent forth that fervent trill;
  'Twas Philomel the song supplying;
And Venus wept, on yonder hill,
  O'er young Adonis, gored and dying.

And then, if perfumed airs came breathing *,
  At eve, from off th' Ægean shore,
While little waves, their white foams wreathing,
  The green-hued deeps were fleecing o'er;
From mountain-cave, beneath the rock,
  'Twas Zephyrus out-sped the breeze;
'Twas Proteus — leading forth his flock
  To feed along the verdant seas.

The Gods — not then they held it scorn
  To mate with old Deucalion's race;
And many a Demigod was born,
  Fit progeny from such embrace.

* This stanza is not in the original.

And deeper faith — intenser fire —
    Fed Sculptor's chisel — Poet's pen;
What nobler themes might Art require
    Than Gods — on earth, and God-like Men?

Yea! Gods then watched with loving care,
    (Or such, at least, the fond belief)
E'en lifeless things of earth and air,
    The cloud — the stream — the stem — the leaf.
Iris — a Goddess! — tinged the flower
    With more than merely rainbow hues;
Great Jove himself sent down the shower,
    Or freshened earth with healing dews.

E'en Beauty's self more beauteous seemed,
    When Ganymede a God could thrall;
And Youth, to fancy, youthlier beamed,
    And Souls were more heroical.

Where Hymen stood for priest, the heart
    In sweeter bonds than our's was wed ;
Nay—life more gently seemed to part,
    When 'twas the Parcæ cut the thread.

And temples shone like palaces,
    And game, and victor's coronal,
And festal dance, 'mid flowers and trees,
    And song and bowl were Sacred—all.
E'en at the last doomed hour of death
    No terrors scared the death-bed room ;
A kiss beguiled the parting breath,
    A Genius welcom'd to the tomb.

If but the willing Graces bent
    O'er deed or rite with smile approving ;
If but the Muses gave consent
    Or cheered, perchance, with accent loving ;

The Gods forebade no pleasure—then—
    Nor doomed it—sin ; nor held it—folly ;
But deigned to share the joys of men ;
    The Beautiful, was still the Holy !

And while those Gods so deigned to share
    Our mortal pleasures, downward bending,
We too to their Empyrean air
    In noble strife were upward tending.
Ah ! generous Creeds, that blossom'd forth
    'Mid southern Græcia's softer bowers,
What blight-wind from our bitter North
    Hath seared your hues and shrunk your flowers ?

Too proud for earlier leading-strings
    Our world disdains each old Ideal ;
And, clogged with mere prosaic things,
    Plods heavily life's sullen Real.

Idalian smiles !   Jove's lofty brow !
   Pan ! the Wood-nymphs ! all are gone !
Bright as ye were, bright Fictions !—now—
   Ye live in Poet's dream—alone.

BROOK OF SANGUINETTO,

NEAR THE LAKE OF THRASYMENE.

WE win, where least we care to strive ;
   And where the most we strive—we miss.
Old Hannibal, if now alive,
   Might sadly testify to this.

He lost the Rome, for which he came ;
   And—what he never had in petto—
Won for this little brook a name—
   Its mournful name of Sanguinetto.

BORDIGHIERA.

(BETWEEN NICE AND GENOA)

RONDEAU.

GRACEFUL Palms of Bordighiera!
Bending o'er the Riviëra;
Tho' by Devon's wave we've seen
Beechen grove, as brightly green;
And the light-leaved linden trees
Quivering in the soft sea breeze;
And have loved them all the more,
Clustering by our native shore;
Yet, ye Palms of Bordighiera!
Bending o'er this Riviëra,
Grove than yours was never fairer—
Graceful Palms of Bordighiera!

ECLIPSE.

Moon! if e'er thy broader light
Helpëd lover's prayer by night;
Now Eclipse hath veiled thee over,
Doubly — doubly — help a lover.
Let thy beams, that shrouded be,
Win to a like mystery.
Now, when stars alone do shine,
Bid my Loved One's brow incline —
Sweet Obscurer! — over mine.
Then, while chaste avowal slips
From her — hereto — guarded lips,
I will bless each bland Eclipse.

Oct. 13. 1837.

ZOË: A PORTRAIT.

WHEN Zoë turns to look or speak,
  We feel a spell the heart beguile.
Dwells it in pure transparent cheek;
  In laughing eye, or frolic smile?

Dwells it in frank, yet well-bred, air;
  Dwells it in habit, choice, but simple;
Lurks it in ringlet of her hair;
  Or shifts it with the shifting dimple?

No!—These are not her spells from Love;
  Only the lesser charms he uses;
Slight witcheries the sense to move;
  His baits—his pitfalls—and his nooses.

Yet these have oft betrayed the wise —
   But she hath deeper spells than these:
A temper, gay as summer skies,
   Yet gentle as the vernal breeze.

And blushes, quick that come — and go,
   As feeling wakens or reposes,
When neck and cheek and forehead glow,
   Like one wide bed of open'd roses.

And ready wit, of playful dealing;
   Or — if some tale of grief betide —
As ready tear; which, while outstealing,
   She — shyly still — attempts to hide.

Ringlets are nets by Cupid spread,
  And such will Abra's prove to thee.
So strong the mesh, tho' fine the thread,
  In vain you'll struggle to be free.

But, soon, like fresh-snared falcon bold,
  Who, fierce at first, his plumage swells,
You too shall learn to love the hold
  Of lady's leash — and hood — and bells.

Or would you flee?   She smiles: secure,
  That, though awhile escaped the chain,
You'll still be watching for the lure
  To perch upon her wrist again.

ON A PICTURE.

THIS pictured work, with ancient graces fraught,
(Or so they say) Albertinelli wrought.
He who that touching piece achieved, where meet
The Sisters twain, in Visitation sweet.
Of which the Tuscan city, 'mid her crowd
Of miracles, e'en yet is justly proud.

Oh! matchless line of years, whose generous strife
Reared the reviving arts to perfect life.
Then Petrarch's native lay refined on love;
Then Angelo the impetuous chisel drove;
Then oracles, that stirred young Raphael's breast,
Spoké forth in colours, clear as words, exprest.

Thou too, the pencil's scarce less gifted seer,

Fair is the dream thy hand interprets here.

How sweet yon infant Christ's down-beaming smile

On bright Saint John; who lifts his own the while!

That bliss of young maternity how sweet!

Where mildly mingling Saint and Mother meet.

Nay, more than mother's rapture; to behold

Her Saviour-Son, by prophet-bards foretold.

Or, if adoring meekness e'er had shrine

In human face, Fond Catherine! 'tis in thine.

In that one present joy of all possest;

Heedless of Future; and by Past—unprest.

But Her's, who stands a-near that elder boy,—

Margaret's—I ween is no untroubled joy.

In Her, methinks, the painter's hand hath sought

Meanings to-plant of more than common thought.

A look, as if that calm, yet clouded, eye
Had glimpsed the minglings of futurity.
And, 'mid the glories of each final doom,
Foresaw, not less, the sorrows first to come.

ON A DOG.

THY happy years of deep affection past,
Cartouche! our faithful friend, rest here — at last.
We loved thee for a love man scarce might mate;
And now we place thee here with sadness, great
As man may own for brute.   Might less be given
To love so pure as thine and so unriven?

  Love was thy very life.   Thine every thought, —
Or instincts — all to that one impulse wrought.
Our words — our very looks — to thee were known;
The shade of feature like the touch of tone.
The pensive brow might some light sorrow press,
(Such as, erewhile, o'er hour of blissfulness

May flit, like summer-cloud, soon come and gone)

'Twas then the lifted eye, and wistful moan,

And head, laid gently on the sufferer's knee,

Told — plain as speech — how sad that grief to thee.

Or did some cheerier look, or word, betray,

How slight soe'er, the sadness passed away ;

Soon the gay bound—fond crouch—or winning whine

As plainly said how much our joy was thine.

That flame of living love, to-day — to-morrow —

The same, thro' circling years of joy or sorrow ;

That even, as revolving years went by,

Seemed but to glow with more intensity,

Say ! could it be created but to die ?

Must man's alone survive his earthly state ?

And all of love beside wheel but a date

Ephemeral — to sink annihilate ?

Vain questionings are these of " Is " or "Ought !"

Oh vain ! perchance unholy strife of thought.

Chase, reasoning Brain ! these doubts that creep and
    steal ;

And cease to think — tho' not ashamed to feel.

MONUMENT AT LUCERNE,

TO THE SWISS GUARD MASSACRED AT THE ASSAULT ON THE
TUILERIES, A.D. 1792.

WHEN madden'd France shook her King's palace floor,
. Nobly, heroic Swiss, ye met your doom.
Unflinching martyr to the oath he swore,
Each steadfast soldier faced a certain tomb.

Not for your own, but others' claims ye died :
The steep, hard path of fealty called to tread,
Threatened or soothed, ye never turned aside,
But held right on, where fatal duty led !

Reverent we stand beside the sculptured rock,
Your cenotaph—Helvetia's grateful stone ;
And mark in wonderment, the breathing block,
Thorwaldsen's glorious trophy — in your own.

Yon dying lion is your monument !
  Type of majestic suffering, the brave brute,
Human almost, in mighty languishment,
  Lies wounded, not subdued ; and, proudly mute,

Seems as for some great cause resigned to die :
  And, hardly less than hero's parting breath,
Speaks to the spirit, thro' th' admiring eye,
  Of courage — faith — and honourable death.

FROM ANACREON.

ODE I.

SING the old Atridæ!
Sing, my Lyre, of Cadmus.
But the Lyre, refusing,
  Only sang of Love.

Strings and Lyre I changed — to
Chaunt of great Alcides.
Still the Lyre responded
  Nought but notes of Love.

Farewell! then — to heroes; —
For what time remains me —
Since my Lyre will echo
  Thoughts alone of Love.

ASTRONOMY.

LUCINDA! Lucinda! why all this abstraction?
　May astronomy hold no communion with mirth?
Stars—comets—eclipses have these such attraction
　To steal you from our mere pleasures of earth?

You, who lately would sportively " flirt it " and " fan
　　it,"
　At dinner or ball—grown so grave in a trice!
Have you found, pretty Plato! so fervid our planet,
　You must needs flee to Saturn to borrow his ice?

Just so it once happened—I well can remember—
　(For seasons, like souls, are erewhile out of tune)
That the frost and the fast-falling sleet of December
　Came to cover the freshness and glory of June.

Like some beautiful prude, all coldness and brightness,
　　The landscape shone chill in its dazzle of snow.
Yet it was but a surface of froreness and whiteness,
　　For green herb and gay flowret were springing
　　　　below.

Till the genial Spirit of Summer, indignant
　　That Winter should thus re-intrude on his reign,
Called Zephyr to aid; and with fervor benignant
　　Woke each valley to gladness and beauty again.

So too, Sweet Astronomer! thou shalt re-waken
　　From these visions remote amid comet and star;
And learn how you truants are ever mistaken
　　Home-pleasures who leave to find new ones afar.

Make but sign from the ark, and each joyful back-comer
　　O'er thy deluge of science shall speed, like the dove.

Fond beamings from friendship unfreeze thee, like
summer ;
   Or, warmer than friendship, some breathing from
   love.

And when—telescope closed—and unpuzzled by Airy—
Thro' opera glass we win pleasanter view ;
Should folk happen to smile at your sky-ward vagary,
   Why—we'll swear that " the stars were in fault,"
   and not you.

EXPERIMENTUM CRUCIS.

WITH different colour glows each ray
That joins to feed the solar day.
Yet, each commingling as they pass,
They lose distinction in the mass,
Where Iris-hues, grown tintless quite,
Stand wondering at their own pure White.

Yet prove that White with sifting lens,
No more if cheats the dazzled sense;
But, re-transmuted to the view,
Beams back its red—or green—or blue.

Nor less, in every church gregarious,
Opinion's colours are as various.

Nor less each hue with other locks,

To form the pure white Orthodox;

That scorns all other shade—sectarian!—

Plain Quaker-drab, or half-tint Arian.

But if—as philosophic use is—

We try Experimentum Crucis;

To find if what so whitely beams

Be, in good sooth, the thing it seems;

From moral lens, in varying streak,

How soon the lines diverge and break!

Observe how rule of faith refracts

From doctrine—here; and, there, from facts.

How many a lurking tinge comes out;

What intersecting lines of doubt.

And that broad stripe of scepticism,

See, how it flashes from the prism.

In prudence, now, we break the glass;
We must view churches but in mass.
Nor split too nicely at the focus
Opinions, jumbled hocus-pocus.

MORAL.

Churches!   Churches! hence take heed;
And give the tolerance which ye need.
Your whitest orthodox effulgence
Worth no one ray—from wise indulgence.

L'ENVOI,

TO A POEM ON TOLERANCE.

Go! little Book, thine own disciple be,

And learn to tolerate those who turn from thee.

Or laughed to scorn, or in oblivion sunk,

Go! little Book, and learn to line a trunk.

Some rain-bound traveller, in ennui's despair,

May cast a moment's notice on thee — there.

Thy last sad hope (and pride deserves such shocks)

Like hers — of old — at bottom of a box.

STEAM TRAVEL.

STEAM TRAVEL.

WHO hath not longed, by converse fired or book,

To break him sudden from his own home-nook,

(There, in cramp nest, too long, like dormouse curled)

And speed from land to land, and scan the world?

But Time and Space stood ready to forbid

Or Niagara — or the Pyramid.

" Soon shall thy arm, Unconquer'd Steam ! afar *

Drag the slow barge and drive the rapid car."

* DARWIN's Botanic Garden, book i.

Some twice five lustres since, so sang the bard :

Bold was the prophecy ; the credence hard.

The jeerer jeered ; the thinker stood aloof

In pause ; " but now the time hath given it
     proof."

Did Venus win from Vulcan, Mighty Power !

That thou shouldst strain a day within an hour?

And lend her thy twin spirits, Force and Speed,

To break down distance for some gentle need?

And did Minerva join Cythera's prayer?

Or bribe thee with some gift of science rare,

For her young sages, or of state or law,

Within vacation half a world to draw ?

And (not as when, of old, men plodded slow

" To Pyrenean or the river Po ")

Fling forth each acolyte, as suits him best,

To Moslem East, or Transatlantic West?

Then snatch the senator, o'er land and main,
Back to his voters and the house — again?

Or from his poetry and picturesque

Whirl back the future chancellor to his desk?

The fire-wheeled bark would part.   Storm saith her
        " Nay "

With blustering throat; yet lo! she bursts away.

In vain around her curl the landward seas;

In vain — to stop her — strains the landward breeze.

Not like yon white winged loiterers, taken aback

By the fierce blast, and foiled of skilful tack;

At anchor tossing still, with close-reefed sail,

Sick of delay, yet bondsmen of the gale;

She, in mad surf tho' forced awhile to reel,

And heave and dive, from bowsprit down to keel,

Asserts, full soon, her self-selected course,

And conquers wind and wave by inner force.

And while swift smoke, as from volcano's mouth,

(Such Pliny saw) is hurried, north or south,

By the head wind; (the swiftlier driven back,

The more to show what power would thwart her track)

She, leaving coast and bay far, far, behind,

As all contemptuous of that bullying wind;

And fluttering round to unresisting spray

Each coming wave, that would contest her way;

Unoared, uncanvassed, marches on, until

Instinct almost she seems with human will.

Like some strong mind, that, shipped on fortune's
          bark,

Holds onward still, unflinching to the mark;

And loves, or so might seem, to breast and urge

Thro' life's worst seas, and scoffs at wind and surge.

But now her prow hath touched the foreign strand;

And harnessed, lo! the iron coursers stand.

Fire hoofed, with fuming nostril; us to bear,

Swift as swift arrow, thro' the whistling air.

We mount the car. And what our course may

     stay,

Strength — Victory — Companions of our way !

On — on we rush. A hundred leagues forecast,

And lo ! a hundred leagues already past.

On — on we rush. A hundred pictures tost

On the quick eye — right — left — and yet not lost.

For as fast eagle, fastest when he flies,

Battle or prey, the things he loves, descries ;

So the brief pictures We ; as sudden caught

By rapid eye for yet more rapid thought.

   And not alone shall glancing vision win

Each larger feature of the sweeping scene,

Wood, stream, or hill ; but many a smaller charm,

Croft, — garden, — lowly roofs of village farm ;

(Which from some causeway lowlier, lovelier seem;

Fond homes for fancy; landscape in a dream;)

With mowers beside their noon-~~day~~ *tide* flagon gay;

And children, tumbling in the tedded hay.

Or—as for contrast—the slow-furrowing plough;

Or feeding kine, that (all accustomed, now)

On as we flash along the echoing ways,

Lift not their quiet heads; but calmly graze.

Tall ship! proud steed! let loftier poets dream;

I plod for thee, most unpoetic Steam!

Thou used, yet scorned! till thro' some chance we find

A poesy in man's all-conquering mind.

SACRED GIPSY CAROL.

GIPSY CAROL.

PROLOGUE.

REFUSE not, Reader, the brief mysterie-play,
  Which our poor Gipsy-trio here enacts;
For thoughtful spirits love such legend lay,
  Oft true to feeling, false albeit to facts.

Nay, judging reason yet more true shall hold
  Such fabling tale, to gentle heart when true,
Than stricter fact, with dogma harsh and cold,
  Oft falsified; to harden me or you.

PROLOGUE.

Faith, like yon liberal sun's impartial power,
  Where'er her genial rays, like his, shall strike,
Wakes forth from every soil its fitting flower;
  If not alike each flower — all flowers — alike.

And tho' erewhile she cleave empyreal air,
  Not less 'mid such as lowly valleys give
She loves to float and pause; and every where,
  Or high or low, in sympathies can live.

Then, thoughtful spirit! hold thou not in scorn
  Her votive gift of very humblest weed.
That humblest weed hath comeliness, where born;
  'Tis still the heart which consecrates the creed.

Nor take our speech in mockery or despite,
  Tho' strange it be, or ruder than thine own.
Where equal justice rules, with equal right
  Each tribe—each tongue—hath access to the
    throne.   **1849.**

SACRED GIPSY CAROL.

CHANSON DES BOHÉMIENS.

STANZA I.

Nous sommes trois Bohémiens, qui devinons

La bonne aventure ; nous sommes trois Bohémiens

Qui dérobons partout où nous sommes.

Enfant aimable et tant doux, mets, mets ici la

Croix (c'est à dire une pièce de monnoie) et

Chacun te dira ce qui t'arrivera.   Commence,

Janan, à lui regarder dans la main.

GIPSY CAROL.

Written in the Provençal dialect, by a priest of Aix, in Provence. Ann. 1680.—See "Millin's Voyage dans le Midi de la France," vol. iv. part 1. page 163.

Millin gives the original Provençal, and also a literal French translation of it, from which latter (here given) the present English translation has been made.

FIRST GIPSY.

GIPSIES Three, Gipsies Three;

Roamers wide o'er field and fell;

Farers free, where'er we be;

Such are we, such are we;

Fortunes also we can tell.

Pretty child! so sweet and mild,

Would you choose your lot to know,

STANZA II.

Tu es, à ceque je vois, egal à Dieu ; et tu es

Son fils adorable.   Tu es, à ce que je vois,

Egal à Dieu ; nè pour moi dans le néant.

L'amour t'a fait enfant pour tout le genre

Humain.   Une vierge est ta mère ; et tu es

Sans père, à ce que parait dans ta main.

Weal or woe — weal or woe —

Cross our hands, for we can show.

Janan! why a-loitering stand?

Come and read the Infant's hand.

SECOND GIPSY.

Thou art, thou art, as I can see,

The equal of the Deity,

His well-belovëd progeny,

   And born to be adored.

Yea—I can see that Thou art He,

Co-partner of the Deity;

Fore-born for me, fore-born for me,

   Ere chaos felt the Word.

For Love it was that gave thee birth;

Boundless Love for All on earth.

With Virgin-Mother — Father — none.

This—all this—in thy palm is shown.

STANZA III.

Il y a encore un grand secret, que Janan n'a

Pas voulu dire ; il y a encore un grand secret,

Qui fera bientôt son effet.   Viens, viens, ici,

Beau Messie ! mets, mets ici la pièce blanche,

Pour nous faire réjouir.   Janan parlera —

Beau Mignon ! mets ici pour dîner.

STANZA IV.

Parmi tant de moyens il y a quelque chose de bien

Fâcheux à faire pour notre bien.   Parmi tant

De choses il y a quelque chose de rigoureux à

Faire pour notre bion.   On y voit une croix pour

FIRST GIPSY.

Yet, still a secret lags behind,

Which Janan hath not cared to tell.

Yet still a secret lags behind,

Which soon shall work its marvel well.

Messiah dear ! put here — put here —

A silver piece, to make us cheer ;

Then — Janan tells it, Darling Dear !

SECOND GIPSY.

Yet, 'mid this bliss, yet mid this bliss,

Something of very hard there is,

   For our behoof, to do.

Yea — yea — I wis, 'mid all this bliss,

Something of very hard there is,

   To work our safety through.

That Cross — Salvation's Cross — I see ;

And if of thy sad martyrie

Le salut de tous ; et, si j'ose te le dirè, la cause

De ton martyre est que tu es trop aimant.

STANZA V.

Il y a encore quelque chose au bout de la ligne

Vitale ; il y a encore quelque chose que je veux te

Dire. Mais, taisons-nous. Viens — viens — bel Enfant,

Donne ici la main, et je vous divinerai quelque

Chose de plus agréable.   Mais, qu'il y ait de

L'argent, car sans cela on ne fait rien.

STANZA VI.

Tu es Dieu et mortel, et, comme tel, tu vivras peu

De temps sur la terre ; tu es Dieu et mortal, et, comme

My tongue the cause may dare to touch,
It is — that Thou hast loved too much.

FIRST GIPSY.

But still at the end of the vital line
A secret untold remains to divine.
Give again, sweet Babe! thy palm to spell,
And a charming secret we can tell.
But, first, the tester we must hold;
Without it, nothing can be told.

SECOND GIPSY.

Thou art God and Mortal too;
And, as such, shalt live — not much —
On this earth, our human birth.
Thou art God and Mortal too;

Tel, tu vivras peu de temps dans notre condition
(C'est à dire, sous la forme humaine).   Mais ta
Divinité est pour l'Eternité.   Tu es l'auteur
De la vie ; et ton essence infinie n'a rien qui soit borné.

STANZA VII.

Ne veux-tu pas que nous disions quelque chose
A ta sainte mère ? Ne veux-tu pas que nous lui
Faisions au moins notre compliment.   Belle Dame,
Venez ici.   Nous connoissons déja que dans votre
Belle main il y a quelque mystère.   Toi, qui es
Si poli, dis lui quelque chose de joli.

And, being so, full soon shalt go

From thy sojourn here below.

Nought a nature, thus divine,

From Eternity can sever;

Endless life a gift of thine,

And thine essence lives for ever.

FIRST GIPSY.

But dost thou not wish, as fit it is,

We should speak a word to thy mother dear;

And in our homely gipsy guise

Make our compliment to her?

Already, fair Lady, we understand

That a mystery lurks in that beautiful hand.

 Do thou, Janan, thou,

 Who so well knowest how,

Say a somewhat to pleasure the lady's ear.

STANZA VIII.

Vous êtes d'un sang royal, et votre maison est

La plus élevée du monde.   Vou êtes d'un sang

Royal, et la votre maison est la plus haute,

A ce que je vois.   Votre Seigneur est votre fils,

Et son père est votre Dieu.   Que pourriez vous

Etre de mieux que la fille de votre maître,

Et la mère de votre Dieu ?

STANZA IX.

Et toi, bon vieillard, qui es là, au coin de la

Crèche ; et toi, bon vieillard, ne veux-tu pas

Que nous voyions dans ta main ? Dis — tu crains,

Peut-être, que nous te dérobions cet âne, qui

SECOND GIPSY.

Lady, thou art of royal blood;

Thy house in glory long hath stood;

 The world hath loftier — none.

Thou art, in sooth, of royal blood,

Thy house in glory long hath stood;

 All this to me is known.

Thy Lord — thy Son! Thy God — his Father!

What would blessed woman rather?

Sainted Daughter of thy Lord!

Happy Mother of thy God!

FIRST GIPSY.

But thou, old Man! who by the manger,

Quietly dost take thy stand,

Let us see, respected stranger,

Let us see and read thy hand.

Est là, détaché.   Noûs déroberions, plutôt, l'enfant

Lui-même.   Mets là-dessus, beau Monsieur ;

Nous n'avons pas encore bu.

STANZA X.

Je vois dans ta main que tu es bien grand ; que

Tu es bien saint —que tu es bien juste.   Je vois

Dans ta main que tu es bien grand, bien juste,

Et bien aimé.   Oh ! divin mari, tu as toujours

Observé une sainte abstinence.   Tu gardes la

Providence.   Ne te garde-t-elle bien ?

And think'st thou, then, that, plotting sly,

We shall steal yon ass that is feeding by?

Old Man! Old Man! far better pelf

Would be the blessed babe himself.

But first, kind Master! hand your groat,

And let us quench a thirsty throat.

SECOND GIPSY.

I see by that hand, I see full sure,

That thou art great and just and pure.

By that hand dost thou stand full clearly proved

Great and pure and well-beloved.

Husband! wisely mastering sense

With a saint-like abstinence,

Thou to Providence didst bow;

And art thou not rewarded now?

STANZA XI.

A présent nous connoissons que tu es venu

Bien pauvre dans le monde. A présent nous

Connoissons que tu es venu sans argent. N'en

Parlons plus; car tu es venu tout nu. Tu craignais,

A ce que nous voyons, le rencontre des Bohémiens.

Qu 'as-tu à craindre, bel Enfant? Tu es Dieu —

Ecoute notre adieu.

STANZA XII.

Si trop de liberté nous a porté à te dire ton

Aventure; si trop de liberté nous a porté

A parler trop librement; nous te prions

Humblement à faire egalement notre bonne

Aventure; et de nous donner une qui dure éternelle-

    ment.

FIRST GIPSY.

But now, Sweet Babe ! full well we wot

That thou art born with little store;

Thy lot—a naked—lowly lot;

Therefore—of pence we talk no more.

And didst thou fear, my darling Dear !

To see the scarecrow gipsy near ?

Yet wherefore start ? for God thou art !—

Then hear our prayer—before we part.

CHORUS OF THE THREE GIPSIES.

If with too much liberty,

We have dared thine ear importune;

If with too much liberty,

We have dared to read thy fortune;

Humbly We pray to Thee,

Build thou for us a destiny;

And be it one, Immortal Son

Blessing us Eternally.

M   Marseilles, 1849.

EPILOGUE TO GIPSY CAROL.

DEVOTION.

WHERE shall Devotion find her fitting food?
   'Twas asked; and it was answered, "Every where."
Whate'er the region, bring but thou the mood,
   And, high or low, her nutriment is there.

Her's—road-side chapel; her's—cathedral roof;
   Her's—Christ—Bambino; her's—Jehovah—King;
The holy reverence, which bends—aloof;
   The love familiar, that delights to cling.

Her's—purest Godhead, veiled in depth of skies;
   The Being, unapproachable—unseen;
And her's — the visible; for peasant eyes
   By village painter robed in red or green.

Come, lead me thou to yonder ancient pile,
   Where the built organ, through its thousand flutes,
Peals majesty; and incense, all the while,
   Is circling up 'mid arches and volutes;

And as we wander thro' the wond'rous fane,
   Or kneel us, trust me! I shall feel, like thee,
Chaunt—censer—picture—statue—rubied pane—
   Nay, cope and robe.   But come thou too, with me,

To where yon worshipper, more picturesque
   Than graceful, in his coat of many a flaw,
Is humbly hymning to that Saint grotesque,
   " From forth his scrannel-pipe of wretched straw."

And then avouch, (not bearing less in mind
   The glorious strains that roll these roofs along,)
That there Devotion too fit food may find
   In the rude notes of that street-chaunted song.

So deemed our elder race.   Their faith — they knew —
   Was strong for daily wear; a stuff to trust.
No flimsy robe, hung up the whole week thro',
   " And but for Sunday-service cleansed from dust ; "

But a stout faith, that free from formalism,
   (On which Devotion's name too oft we dub,)
In week-day life nor found, nor sought, a schism;
   But mingled with it; and could bear the rub.

Or, must we come in smoother phrase array'd,
   (Tho' truth, I ween, might spare such silken grace,)
Their faith (like Una, wheresoe'er she stray'd)
   Could make "a sunshine in the shady place."

And far above, as abstract thought may reach,

    And far beneath, as human instincts go,

Could find congenial atmosphere in each;

    No theme too lofty, as no love too low.

With such interpretation would I leaven

    That ladder-vision, erst by Jacob seen;

Its foot on common earth; its top in heaven;

    And God's mild angels on each step between.

                             1849.

TRUTH.

"Truth may lie fossil in some cave, no doubt;
But 'twere a mad success to win her out."
Rhymed Plea for Tolerance.

A STRIPLING Bonze (from Eastern clime
  We bring the tale we have to tell)
Was standing, once upon a time,
  Beside the margin of a well.

Down which he peer'd him wistfully,
  As if all deeply pondering
On matter which therein might be,
  Some curious or some precious thing.

There while he paused, an old Fakir
  Observing, as he wandered by,
Thus spake him, "What dost thou do here?
  To whom the stripling made reply.

"Good Father! I have heard them tell
    How truth, our angel-friend in doubt,
Doth hold her dwelling in a well,
    And I full fain would win her out."

"Nay, prythee, Boy! lift not that rope,
    If grey experience may advise.
The very best we e'er may hope
    From truth, when won, is compromise."

"Or, scorning that, make sure, fond youth!
    Thou now art sowing years of strife.
Who needs will battle for the truth
    Shall lead a mighty sorry life."

The stripling heard; the rope let go;
    And never from that hour applied
To such unthankful task; and lo!
    Became Chief Bonze before he died.

TIME.

LIKE as one, erewhile pursuing,
   Shouts him o'er his captured foe,
" Spite of all thy fleetest doing,
   Now, thou Slave! behind me go."

So doth Time, austere transmuter,
   Following, following, fast and fast,
Lay strong hand on forward Future ;
   Then consigns him to the Past.

MEMENTO VIVERE.

WHEN life was young, in pensive guise
   I made it a fantastic glory,
To pause and sentimentalize
   O'er every sad " Memento Mori."

Dear fourscore friend! in their dull place
   How gladlier now I turn to thee,
With all thy cheery wit and grace,
   Thou bright " Memento Vivere."

AGE.

FULL oft you're plaining that in age
  Our faculties and feelings die.
And it may be that thinkers sage
  Do think like you.   Yet plain not I.

When sick we've grown of pride and show,
  Why should our striving strength live on?
Or why should love forbear to go,
  When all we cared to love—are gone?

GOSSIP.

Gossip right and left you're strowing,
   Never heeding what you do ;
Tho' each idle word you're sowing
   Friend and neighbour long may rue.

When we marked you lately loosing
   Stone from yonder green hill's side,
You but in your sport were choosing
   Swift adown to see it glide.

You look'd pale tho', when in fury,
   Like a mad thing just releas'd,
Threatening work for judge and jury,
   Wild it whirred o'er man and beast.

Think then, Chatterer ! 'mid your doing,
   If for others nought you rue,
How the very seed you're strewing
   May spring up—ill seed for you.

Yon maim'd traveller, you behold him,
   Smitten sore by avalanche;
Wiser heads in vain had told him
   On to move, in silence staunch.

Now his own sad cup he's drinking;
   Word of his provoked the fall,
Which so lamed; and left him thinking
   How that word was cause of all.

WINDS OF DOCTRINE.

By winds diverse of doctrine blown,
   Old Spurio, lately bigot fix'd,
Hath now no creed to call his own,
   But slants him on, some two betwixt.

So when, cross-meeting, force and force
   Have smote some stationary ball,
It takes no longer straightway course,
   But sidles to diagonal.

CASA MIA.

" Casa mia, casa mia,
    Per piccina che tu sia,
    Tu mi pari una badia."

THOU wert born where huge Missouri,
    Rushing heretofore alone,
Bears to Mississippi dowry
    Of more waters than his own ;
But hast never learn'd, like me,
From the years of infancy,
With unsated love to look
On one own dear little brook.

Thou hast felt the treeless prairie
    In its awful sameness spread ;
Countless leagues, that never vary ;
    Wide well nigh as ocean's bed ;

But hast never learned, like me,

From the years of infancy,

How to prize the hedge-row bound

Of one tiny plot of ground.

Thou hast dreamed where endless forest

   Clusters on, a realm of trees ;

And, to hear thee, half abhorrest

   Any woods less vast than these ;

For thou ne'er hast learned like me,

From the years of infancy,

How to love, with love unbroke,

Some one tree, this own old oak.

Vaunt thou then, if such thy notion,

   Prairie — forest — flung afar ;

And thy streams, whose mighty motion

   Meets the tides with equal war ;

But accord meanwhile to me

What I've loved from infancy,

This one tree — this hedge-row nook —

And my own dear little brook.

Holly Bush, Oct. 1848.

TRANSLATION.

INVENI portum.   Spes et Fortuna valete;

Sat me lusistis; ludite nunc alios.

I've found a port.   Hope — Fortune — Farewell ye !

Cheat others now.   Enough ye've cheated me.

N

GRAMMARYE.

" Argantyr! awake — awake —
 Hervor bids thy slumbers fly.
 Magic chords around thee break ;
 Argantyr! reply — reply."

IN vain had they striven — those Beldames three —

With all their might of grammarye,

And many a mutter and many a hum,

To make the Dead Man from his tomb forth come.

For they had vowed by force of spell,

The reason why I dare not tell,

To drag him once more to light of day,

And bring him far and far away

From that his silent house of clay :

Which, ere he came there, in grave-clothes dress'd,

He had sighed for, so oft, for his home of rest.

" Away, away, ye Mumblers three!

Away, quoth the Wizard, and leave him to me!

Ay, leave him to me, and I'll play him a stave,

That, I warrant, shall force him to stir in his grave,

And fumble from 'neath his coffin lid,

And, up, follow me wheresoever I bid."

" But first, ye old Hags! go bring me my viol,

Which from Living—nor Dead—brooked never denial.

And my bow, which I strang, to suit such song,

Of a drowned witch's locks, both lank and long.

And deep howsoever his grave it may be,

Were it deep as a well, he shall list him to me."

They have tottered them back and brought him the
      viol

Which from Living—nor Dead—brooked never denial;

And they cower them close to witness the trial;

Grinning and gibbering " Now we shall see

If he, with his stave, doeth better than we."

And that magical viol, oh ! how was it made ?

From a gibbeted skull which the winds had flayed

Of its dark flowing locks and each crinkle of skin,

Brown-shiny without, and hollow within.

With eye-holes for sound-holes; with neck-bone for
                neck ;

While the strings to bridge up 'twas the nose gave its
                wreck.

For, somehow or other, nose, mouth, brow and chin,

Each ghost of a feature chimed wond'rously in,

To fashion the form of that strange violin ;

Which, looking its player full up in the face,

Would mock him, erewhile, with a wicked grimace,

As much as to hint " Ere 'tis long — in my place."

Yet the Wizard — he bated no jot of his pride ;

But smiled him in triumph the head-stone beside.

For he felt 'neath his bow the throb of the stave

All eager to summon the Dead from his grave.

Then thus to his mocker, " To-day I sway thee ;

Come to-morrow what will — 'tis small matter to

me."

And he bade forth the song.   Nor sad — nor slow —

Like prophet's, who, constrained to show,

Reluctantly denounceth woe ;

But brisk, as in merriment on it did go,

And we knew he was gibing the sleeper below.

And we saw, ere 'twas long, the round turf up-

ride,

And split in the middle and fall on each side ;

And lo ! on his feet the Dead Man stood !

First — pausing awhile, as in puzzled mood,

Then — followed wherever the Wizard would.

While those Beldames three, in hideous glee,

Shouted and laughed the sight to see.

PUNNING—AFTER COWLEY.

TO AQUILIUS.

PUN and Wit do both surprise;
  Yea, but with a difference.
Offspring foolish—offspring wise—
  This—of sound; and that—of sense.

Easy pun, like plaister mould,
  E'en when best, may scarce assure a
Fragile fame; while Wit doth hold
  Bravely on, piëtra dura.

Yet when Pun to Wit allied,
  Close to Wit doth take his station,
Why, his presence we'll abide
  For the sake of his Relation.

Or when thou thro' every fytte

　　Dear Aquilius ! hast been running ;

Wisdom — poetry — and wit,

　　Then dost drop to sheerest Punning.

Tho' with sound he ill agree ;

　　Tho' with sense sad war he wage ;

Still we'll greet him for his glee ;

　　And love him for his parentage.

TO A FEMALE FRIEND,

RETURNING TO AMERICA.

LADY ! you ask a farewell verse;
  Reluctant I obey.
Far, gladlier far, would we rehearse
  Some rhyme to bid thee stay.
For, if but lately we have met,
We all shall lose thee with regret.

But if full surely thou must go
  From us, who fain would keep,
May westering breezes cheerly blow,
  Rewafting o'er the Deep
To where thine own dear land imparts
Its bliss of loved and loving hearts.

Of late, like some full cargoed ship,
   Thy mind did voyage forth ;
Transporting on no vulgar trip
   Its freight of precious worth ;
And bartering on, from shore to shore,
Or thought for thought, or lore for lore.

Yet tho' from Gaul and Rome's own clime
   Rich memories thou hast borne
For home-reflection's after-time,
   I know thou wilt not scorn
To muse erewhile on Britain's bowers ;
Thy native land scarce less than ours.

Blood, that was once our English blood,
   No more let seas divide.
A mightier power hath stemmed the flood,
   The old Atlantic tide ;

And wide and wider hence shall roll
The glorious traffic — soul with soul.

Lady ! not easily withstood !
  Thy frolic wish is won ;
And, if in somewhat pensive mood,
  Behold five stanzas done.
But, Lady ! only come agen,
For stanzas five — we'll write thee ten.

PAST AND FUTURE.

PAST AND FUTURE.

Our Past—how strangely swift! Its years—mere
    months!

Months — clipped to weeks! and longest day— an
    hour!

But oh! how slow the Future; slow to all

Of every age and being.   Yon school-urchin,

Fresh from his Christmas-home, as now he bends him

With saddened brow o'er the black greasy slate;

Or strains himself, at stroke of early clock,

His all-unwelcome bedtime, to confront

Cold touch of wiry sheet, ah! not like home's;

How vainly would he pierce the dim half year

To his next holidays; and asks himself,
" And will they—will they—can they ever come?"

   Youth too, who sighs for the proud masterdom
Of one and twenty; his great holiday;
When he may satisfy intense desire
With horn and hound and golden racing-cup;
Maturer toys!   Or he, young too, who wends him
From Eastern warfare, on some gallant ship,
Home to his bride affianced, whom he hath loved
From their late school-hood; tho' the willing prow
Cut cheerily on; and the still-steady breeze
Stiffen each sail; and that long lively wake
May tell to all but him how fast she goes;
He too (and each in turn) exclaims " How slow!"

   Yea, Middle-Age not less, tho' oft he hath proved
How Time, the crawling tortoise, as he deemed,

Hath, all that while, been Time, the fleet of foot;

Who—having won the Future all too soon—

With sudden turning, as of wheel reversed—

Unwinds that Future back into the Past;

Spite of experience, he too holds the Coming

A long, long tract; blank space interminable,

On which to inscribe his plans; wealth to be won;

Or honours added; or field joined to field;

Or glory achieved thro' arms, or art, or song;

Till, on a day, he finds his head a-whitening;

Yet, even then, his plans all unfulfilled,

May scarce yield credence to his own grey hairs.

So surely is the Future long to All!

Nay, not to All.   A certain hill there is,

Not like the mighty Tuscan's obscure wood,

" In the mid-way of this our mortal life,"

But one third further on; which whoso climbs,

Should pensive thought disown him not, there finds

If brief the Past, how brief the Future too.

Thence marks he what scant slip doth lie between

Him and that fated sea, that gulfeth all.

So near, he views distinct the thin surf-line,

Narrowing yet more and more the narrow strand.

And even may hear the onward-stealing wave,

Which pulses, ah! how regular; if faint

As his own pulse, which soon shall cease to beat.

Sad lore to learn! which he, who once hath learned,

Forgets not; but henceforward walks his life

Ghost-beckoned by the Future.   Like to him,

(Of such men tell) some second-sighted seer,

For whom the very merriest village bells,

That ever pealed for new-born babe, or bride,

Have yet, within, a haunting under-note,

That saith "Ere long we toll."   Or yet more like

Yon felon-wretch law doomed; to whom yet mercy

Hath granted some brief respite; if, in sooth,

It be a boon of mercy, that sad leave

To pause awhile, and shudder o'er th' abyss,

And then "Farewell."

               So 'tis—that every age

Doth make its own believings.   Things, so named,

But seemings; and our very solidest facts

Mere shadows from the will; or standing-place

Shapes the whole vision.   Sculptor young was he,

And teeming with the thoughts of his own years,

Who first devised yon figure of old Time.

He knew him old; and gave him withered limbs;

Yet sinewy, and strong for work withal;

(For Youth believeth in long working day,)

And those firm wings; for he had far to fly;

And that stout scythe; for he had much to mow;

Then with one forelock, and ('twas Art's caprice)

A chrystal hour-glass in the marble-hand,

The statue stood complete.

              And stood around

A group—as young—regarding.   Hopes and Fears—

Nay—Fears were none; but gratulating Hopes;

Each for his own glad prospect.   While the gayer

Were jeering him.   As "Go thy way, Old Grey-beard!

Thou of the chrystal cone admonitory!

With thy long scythe and longer wings, go mow

All, if thou wilt, the steppes of Tartary;

Or fly thee, if thou choose, from pole to pole;

For what art thou to us?   Unless indeed

We clutch—as sooth we will—the jocund moral

Of thy short forelock, and enjoy the Present."

That Present long had passed.   Years were flown by;

And lo! there stood beside that self-same statue

Another group; another yet the same;

A few grey-headed men; the scant remains

Of those who had gazed before. The rest—where
    were they?

But now, methinks, not only were their locks,

But eye-sights changed,—to which no more appeared

The same—that statue; or had changed, like them.

For that broad chrystal cone, down which, of old,

When shifted to reverse by curious hand,

The sands had seemed to drawl, (like some rich un-
    guent

From forth the narrow neck of golden vase

Dripping reluctantly, when dark-locked beauty

Impatient craves it for her clustering hair,)

They now beheld it dwarfed and tapered down

To minute-glass; through which the glittering grains,

Too swift almost for aged eyes to follow,

Leapt twinklingly ; as if in turn to jeer,

With " Now, good friends ! we sure run fast enough !"

So too that scythe, whose length of curvature

Had seemed full fit to sweep uncounted fields,

(And which, or whether plied thro' rough or smooth,

— For rough and smooth to Time are all the same —

Had stirred the heedless ear of youth no more

Than doth the mower's, who, on some sweet June morn,

Steals silently amid the dewy grass,)

Was now a short hooked sickle ; fit not less

For its cramped breadth of harvest ; and they heard it,

Or thought they heard it, rasping audibly

With brisk sharp rustle 'mid the dry sere stalks ;

Themselves as dry and sere !

                                While each long wing,

Down pointed from spare back to skinny heel,

—Which might have borne strong eagle on his quest

From realm to realm—was clipped and rounded now,

As those which only just suffice to bear

The whirring partridge on from brake to brake;

If swift, yet soon to fall.   Or like the plumes .

Fan-shaped and hardly fledged; which sculpture hangs

On the sleek shoulders of the little Loves.

They too, as many a maiden's tear attests,

They too, who take short flights—and drop too soon.

But lo ! beside that figure of old Time

Stood now another figure; which, whilom,

Had not stood there; or which they saw not then,

When youth is busied more to feel than see.

Figure it was with loosely-folded arms,

And bended brow, and introspective eye,

Which seemed as if it pondered on the Past.

The young, had any such been mingling there,

Might well have marvelled what such form should
　　mean.

But of that gray-haired group, which clustered round,

Not one there was but knew the name—and sighed—

When —asking—it was answered them " Regret."

1849.

ASPASIA.

TO ———.

BRIGHT Aspasia! say — how is it?
  Tell us with what spell is rife
Smile of thine, whose briefest visit
  Wakes each dullest clod to life?

Zephyr shall we type thee, thawing
  Vernal flower from Arctic block?
Or some Attic sun-beam, drawing
  Hidden oil from rudest rock?

Or believe thee sprite of ages?
  Very Her, whom Socrates
Worshipped more than all the Sages,
  All the vaunted Seven of Greece.

And their systems throwing over
   For the lessons of her eyes,
Happy pupil! happier lover!
   Doubly won his name of " Wise."

So come thou, delicious preacher!
   Orator—of sparkling looks !
Come, like Her, and be our teacher;
   Better far than all the books.

Book-worm pedants but benight us;
   Cumbrous setting clouds the gem.
Bring but thy bright smile to light us,
   And who'd go for fogs to them?

HINT TO POETS.

BROTHER Bard! if dream thou nourish,
  Thro' new fancy or new truth,
'Mid the sons of fame to flourish,
  Thou must lean on heart of youth.

Youth is eager; youth — elastic;
  Plieth both to old and new.
Age deems all, but old, fantastic;
  And doth " novel gauds" eschew.

Youth, as yet of time unthrifty,
  Poet's song will stay to hear.
Bent on business grey-beard Fifty
  To the charmer stops his ear.

Bring us back your wandering Homer !

Glorious pedlar—poem-pack'd !

Midas old shall greet the Roamer

With a clause from Vagrant Act.

Count not on your fresh creation !

Living Homer begged his bread.

'Twas a second generation

Twined its wreath for Homer—dead.

RAISING THE DEAD.

RAISING THE DEAD.

WE all have heard, and marvelled as we heard,
Of seers, who have raised the Dead from out their tombs,
And made them parley.   Nor would I gainsay
Such story.   For who knows the invisible links,
Mysterious sympathies of life with life,
Or life, perchance, with death ?   Or guesses what
Thessalian spells, or what divining rod
The soul erewhile may have weird gift to use,
And, with strange power, interrogate the grave,
Yet leave the turf unbroke?   Or even may reach
Up the blue regions, where freed spirits dwell,

With her far-finding telescope of love;
Or, may be, hate !

                    Nay, are our nightly dreams
But fancies of the brain ? some straggling shreds
From memory ? or, meaner still, mere jet
From stomach or nerve ?   Or, rather, do we not,
(So sometimes I have deemed) what time we sleep,
— If sleep it be, and not a wider waking —
Within the close-drawn curtains, face to face,
Hold actual commerce with the living Dead?
Who stand beside us ; and do look upon us ;
And well nigh touch us with their stony hands ;
And see themselves in our fixed lineaments :
Fit comradeship ! dead life with living death !
And then, when morn hath come, with crow of cock,
Or early swallow, twittering by the lattice,
To summon them back to their lonely homes,

And us to all the over busy doings
Of this world's life; we, in our ignorance,
Because they have left no foot-prints on the night,
Do swear we have dreamed.

Nor doth it hap alone
Within the silent and the dim domain
Of sleep; that doubtful confine laid between
The Here and the Hereafter; nor where deed
Of guilt doth hold some troubled mind awake
At midnight; nor where mist, obscure as night,
Hath wrapt the Gaël upon his mountain moor,
And the pale wraith doth prophesy him woe;
Not in such moments only do the Dead
Revisit earth.   Go thou and throw thyself
On some hill side, beneath the bluest sky
And cheeriest sun; or — better — when the touch
Of twilight eve hath sanctified the air,

P

And very earth thou liest on; and surrender

Thy spirit to old memories; and 'tis chance

If then thy half-closed eyes behold them not.

Uncalled they come; or led by threads of thought

Too fine to scan.   Thy dearest objects once,

And now, behold! they come to thee again,

And hang around thee, sweetly visible,

And real as life itself.   If life itself

Be a real thing; and not—as some have deemed—

A dream of shadows; sequel to a drama

Acted before; and we (its actors, then,

But, now, forgetful of the parts we played)

No creatures of fresh breath, but the stale ghosts

Of former Being; doomed to walk once more

This weary earth; and fret the appointed years,

In penance of some evil we have done;

But when — and what — and where — we must not
        know.

Uncalled they come.   But we can call them too,
(I speak but what I know) and make them pass
Before us.   If not alway, yet by fits,
When the strong will and planet hour have met
In apt conjunction.   But why only then,
Or not to all accorded, who may find?

Then may be seen the newly-gifted seer,
With steadfast eye, yet outward nought beholding,
Like one in presence of some lofty thought
Or deed; absorbed in it, and it alone;
Or prophet so may have gazed in his strong hour.
For now he feels his spirit privileged
All strangely (how — he knows not, yet he knows it)
To hold communion with the parted life;
And from that very spot where now he stands,
To speed (as if along some chargèd wire,

That mocks at far and near, and rough and smooth)
His swift invisible message to the tomb.

    I speak but what I know.   Of late I found me
Where I had dwelt of yore; and stood to gaze
On the once well-known scene.   Behind me rose
The quaint old town; its square cathedral tower
Lifted above; while all before and round
Lay spread the lovely landscape.   Those smooth meads;
And the bright sparkling river, bright as ever,
Gliding amid; and bearing white-sailed bark
To the near sea.   And green hills sloping up
On the other side; with woods and homes ancestral;
And many a cheery prospect-tower, that told
How man had loved the region; and the purple
Of heathy moors beyond them.   And I thought me
Of all their little valleys, folded in;
Each with its vagrant brook.   Sweet solitudes!

Which I had roamed with Her, who made them all
Sweeter than solitude; from whom I had dreamed
Never to part.   But on that baffled vision
I dared to think no more.

                              Yet still I longed
To muse on some whom I had known — with Her —
In that spring-hour of life, (They were not all
Deceivers !) and who now, like Her, were gone !
And never on this earth to meet again,
Save only in such vision — memory-led.

So, all the less disturbedly to dream,
I stood and leaned, with closëd eyes, against
That lingering fragment of the old town-wall,
Where I had leaned of old — but not alone !
And memory came to aid me, the whole spot
Re-peopling; and I caught, or seemed to catch

Familiar looks; and heard, or seemed to hear,

Familiar tones; first—one's; and then—another's.

The best beloved came first.   Relations dear,

Part of whose life I was, as they of mine;

And friends—as dear.   And then acquaintances,

More or less strict.   And foremost among these,

(For now—as then—the church had due precedence)

The well-bred dean; and jovial prebendary;

And wife prebendal, with her stately look

Dwarfing wife secular.   And, next, town-member,

From his near seat, aye welcome; liberal ever

Of hare and pheasant; or with blandest smile

Winning constituent.   And young barrister

From the great city; at provincial board

Predominant; with legal tale and jest

From Westminster or circuit.   And the staid

Physician; and the brisk apothecary,

Rapping from door to door; with news from each

Regaling convalescent.   Gossip rare !

Yet kindly ever by the poor man's bed.

There too the youthful curate, with white brow

And chiselled lip; and mild, yet fervent eye;

Full oft descanting with ingenuous warmth

On type or prophecy; while hectic cheek

All the sad time too plainly spoke its own.

    Now wherefore was it ? (for I sought it not)

That on a sudden stretched its length before me

The old town ball-room; lit as it was wont

At races or assize time.   And behold!

Thro' the wide double doors came flitting in

Fair white-robed Misses; separate or in bevies;

Now, ones—and twos—and threes; then, thick toge-
      ther,

(Like gradual snow flakes) whitening the whole floor.

Or rather shall we say, for fitter type,

Like orange-blossoms, which some summer-breeze
Is fluttering from amid the glossy boughs
To blanch the beds beneath.   So in they streamed,
A galaxy of muslin.

     Those white robes
Had long been shrouds! and that gay dance — what
  since,
Let Holbein tell us!

      Yea, I saw them all,
As I had seen of yore.   Here the young heir,
Not quite unconscious.   There, the matron-mother
Of those three youthful Graces; eagle eyed;
From the side benches, her tall eyrie, brooding
O'er park and manor.   And flirtations thin,
Meant for the general eye; and deep-souled looks
Of silent love, the lookers fain would hide.

And wreathëd smiles — some, hollow; and the sneer
Forecast to wound; and petty rivalries,
And pettier leagues; and all the worthless doings
Of this our daily life — done by the Dead!

Them too I saw, those three deep-wrinkled hags,
Pink-rouged; dark-ringletted; and diamond-decked;
Yet hag-like still.   Beneath whose baleful breath
The fairest fame would wither; whose dim hints,
And counsels shrewd, and worming confidences
Had art to melt the firmest plighted faith
Of youthful bride affianced.   There they stood,
With snake-like eyes; sharp voices; finger up;
Those ball-room beldames! And I heard them gibber,
E'en as ghosts gibber; or as they themselves
Had gibbered here on earth.   I heard, and scarce
Forbore to curse them.

　　　　　　Say, had wrath such power

To quicken memory? for it now seemed freshened

To a new strength.　We all have read, when earthquake

Hath smote some ancient city's street of tombs,

Disrupting their foundations, how come forth

Graven sarcophagus, and pictured urn,

And the grey ashes of forgotten men

Five hundred lustres buried.　Even so,

Stirred by some influence, be it what it might,

Did now the long-sealed chambers of the brain

Give up their Dead.　And, lo! before me stood

All of the Parted I had known from when

I first began to know; (for of the Quick

None came to mingle).　And not those alone

Whom I had sought to see, but all, yea all,

Or separate, or in clusters.　Mother — nurse —

Preceptor.　Next, school-comrades — college-friends —

(Ah! little had we dreamed to part so soon)

And then the yet more numerous host, 'mid whom
Our after-life hath thrust us.   More and more,
Swifter and swifter.   Till there grew a sense
Confused and ill at ease, as if it now
Were all too cramp for those who there would enter.

    Hast thou not heard erewhile some gentle music?
(If thro' similitudes I speak (perchance,
Usque ad nauseam) 'tis that speech direct
Might fail to tell my story ; nor boast I
Wide masterdom of words.)   But as some music,
Slowly preluding with soft notes and few,
Swells by degrees ; and other instruments
Join in ; till finally the whole orchestra,
Like some freshed river, swollen with tributaries,
Hath gathered up the multitudinous minglings, .
Then flings them all with unresolvable speed
In one broad crash upon the shrinking ear ;
So shrank I at that moment, as all these,

Poured forth from East and West and North and South,

Were round and round me eddying, till the brain spun.

   Nor was I any longer in the Present;

(For time itself seemed reeling with the brain)

My Present was the Past! Life's actual hour

Supplanted by the vanished! As they tell

Of drowning men, with whom all former memories;

All they have done or suffered; known or felt;

Childhood and manhood; loves and enmities;

Nay, things that were, or seemed to be, forgotten,

Are all whirred back upon the sharpened sense,

To be compressed within that struggling minute;

Thus suddenly, (I may not say unrolled,

But, somehow, flung before me) in that instant

Flashed a whole life.

              How may words paint to thee

What thou hast never felt? Or how I stood

(There was no time for fear) but all-amazed,

Like one who hath oped a sluice he may not stop.

Till, in a moment of collected will,

Quivering the while, but stronger than I knew,

I bade them — and they went !

                                   What went ? mere visions ?

Were these, so real, so distinct, but visions ?

Or were they — could they be (I dare confess

Such thought was glancing by me) no — not shadows !

But they — the Dead — come back in body again ?

    " Yea, visions " — thou wilt tell me — " shadows

        mere —"

" Such stuff as dreams are made of;" when the mind

Diseased, or else in sport, is peopling space

With shapes of matter. (If that mind and matter

In sooth be twain.) Or thou wilt tell how fancy

Is still most potent when the soul is stirred ;

As mine was then.   Or else wilt hold wise descant,

In metaphysic guise, of filmy links

Associative ; and echoes — tho' unheard —

From thought to thought.   And think'st thou then
        that I

Not thus philosophized ?   Yet 'twas not these :

I speak but what I know — and 'twas not these.

    Now listen to a tale incredible !

And yet most true.   Nay, 'tis no jesting story ;

Nor was I drugged with opium ; nor was it

Some wild hallucination of a brain,

Thou'lt say — o'erwrought.   But it was given me,

(I tell thee a true tale, believe or not)

But it was given me in that hour to know

Distinct, as e'er distinctest knowledge stood,

(Yet how or whence such knowledge came, I knew not ;

Nor if to tempt or punish, that I know not ;)

But it was given me in that hour to know

That they, the Parted—wheresoe'er they were—

That they should feel and hear me in their graves !

Not merely in yon church-yard, but wherever

Their bones did house them.   And should leave awhile,

(No, not mere phantoms, but the very Dead)

Those graves all tenantless — to march before me !

  'Twas a strange power.   A ghastly dream to shrink
      from,

If it had been a dream ; but, being a power,

I cared to use it ; and with will perverse

(For power corrupteth will), did choose to see

Her, whom but now my heart had shrunk to think of.

And She did come ! and I beheld her what

She was when last we parted.   Was it love

Or anger made me call that vision up?

I might not stay to know; but this I know;

That all of wrath, long cherished—and revenge—

(For that thought too, all hideous as it was,

Had yet been there) did melt them fast away

Before that once loved presence; till (each wrong

Forgiven) the old affection ruled alone.

One other was there in that church-yard laid,

Whom I had loved the least (why did She love him?)

My foe; and him—the next—I willed to see.

And will was now compulsion; and I saw him;

Yea, with these very bodily eyes I saw him

Stir in his shroud, beneath the coffin-lid!

And staring upward with wide helpless eyes,

He moaned—I heard him—wherefore dost thou wake

      me?

Then too I saw—nay 'twas no fantasy—

Two other eyes—eyes unmistakeable—

Gazing reproachfully.   And all at once,

With a most swift revulsion of the heart,

I started from my own unnatural power,

And knew that I had done a deed unholy.

Ay, started every limb; and so aroused me!

And, lifting with that start the closëd lids,

Beheld, oh blessed! just beneath me lying

That alway lovely landscape; lovelier now

Than ever; while, like ghost before the day,

The unholy power had vanished.

                   As some dreamer,

Amid the wanderings of his troubled dream,

All on a sudden finds himself in-coiled

In some strange guilt; tho' how it was he knows not;

Nor even if his; yet, nathless, shame and fear

Are all around him; if by chance, just then,

From forth the sweetly dawning East, some ray

Slant to his eye-lids, heavenly visitant!

He, leaping up with inexpressible joy,

Finds himself shrieved; or as some noble spirit,

Who, lured by pride, (oh! if such tale be true,

May heaven from us avert the dire temptation)

Hath plighted with the Demon, dreadful pact!

And sold his soul for power; and, having tested,

Succeeds; then shudders at his own success;

And flings him on his kness in agony

Of prayer; if that, with penitence, may melt

The seal from off the accursed bond; and lo!

His prayer is heard.   Like him — like him so saved

In such a mortal hour, ev'n so felt I;

When, starting from that gift of horrible might,

(Or be it dream, if dream thou still wilt have it)

I did behold again the cheery sun

On that up-sparkling river.   Mother Earth!

To me thou ne'er wert dearer.   Rather say,
Never so dear.   Oh! how I joyed to see
Those blue-eyed children, lightly gamboling
On the shorn turf anear.   That loving dog,
Who seemed as if he ne'er could love enough,
Fond frolicking beside them; every bird,
How small soever, that with tiny rustle
Burst from the bushes.   Ay, and those grave daws,
Now, musing on the old cathedral tower;
Now, wheeling round and round in the clear air.

Oh! what a calming bliss to be once more
(Escaped such fearful fact — or mocking vision)
Amid these mild realities of life!
.Then first it was I comprehended how
Complacently might king resign his crown.
Nor marvelled any longer at the tale
Of potent wizards, who had burned their books.

1849.

NOTES.

NOTES.

A DAY AT TIVOLI.

WHILE choosing the old heroic couplet for his vehicle, the author has been fully aware how little popular that measure is. One cause of this may be its presumed want of variety. And where (as Cowper has said, speaking of Pope) "every warbler has the tune by heart;" where the writing has been a mere imitation; a writing, after a recipe; the objection is, no doubt, well founded.

But where the thought or the feeling shall honestly have dictated the versification (which fact would include cadence, tone of expression, and also length of paragraph) it would seem that there might be variety sufficient. At all events the writer has chosen this measure as best fitted for his particular purpose. Not assuredly for its easiness of execution. For by him, who aspires to write the couplet as it ought to be written, it will be found by no means so easy as the looser lyric.

Page 5.   Line 5.

All strangely perforate too, with rounded eyes.

Such perforations characterize old olive trees, and to an imaginative observer may well suggest the notion of being watched.

Page 6.   Line 10.

How falls or winds each little cascatelle.

" The cascatelle, or little cascades, inferior in mass and grandeur, but equal in beauty to the great fall." — EUSTACE.

Page 14.   Line 7.

To face, in ship, the deadly Afran breeze.

Let this line recal to the thought of some, into whose hands the present poem will fall, the loved and respected name of the late Commodore William Jones, who commanded the Penelope on the coast of Africa, and died a victim to the climate.

Page 24.   Line 3.

Or cruel bandit plants him, &c.

See " Three Months passed in the Mountains East of Rome," by Maria Graham.

Page 24.   Line 7.

Thou pausest for a while in silent lake.

The Anio forms three lakes in its course.

Page 24.   Line 18.

Which here he loved to weave (or so they say).

This is a common, but probably not a well-founded, tradition.

Page 27.   Line 4.

Here, where ten centuries do not make the Old.

He who has journeyed in classical lands will recal the several and varying estimates, which, as modified by locality, he has been led to make of time.   If he be a native of northern Europe his antiquities will have been, chiefly, mediæval and ecclesiastical ; and, when at Rome, he will probably have desired to see some church or baptistery of Constantine or Helen ; or to dive into the catacombs for records of the early Christians.   Already his mediæval antiquities will have lost some part of their savour.   But as, next day, he meditates in the forum, Helen and Constantine and the catacombs have in turn faded down.   And as he stands by the Cloaca Maxima, or gropes through the Mammertine prisons, then the forum itself is of dwindled antiquity.

In Greece he is passingly told by his Cicerone not to trouble himself about such or such a wall.   " It is merely Roman ! "   And should he afterwards chance to find himself in presence of the Ægyptian Memnon, he cannot but think with what contempt that venerable statue, if still vocal, would speak of Greece, " the up-start ! "

"Ask where's the North? At York — 'tis on the Tweed.
In Scotland — at the Orcades; or — there —
At Greenland — Zembla — or the Lord knows where."

POPE.

Page 27. Line 13.

As Ciceroni teach us — or beguile. ·

There are two diminutions of the pleasure of seeing ancient Rome. The one, that the ruins are often so much ruined, that it is not easy to make out what they originally were. This however might well be borne with, if the traveller were only allowed to remain in that state of passive doubt, not altogether unpleasing, under which he asks himself, "If knowledge or if mystery please the most."

But now comes the second diminution. He continually finds himself involved in some battling controversy between opposing claims; what this antiquary stoutly asserts that other denying as stoutly — and this is more or less — a vexation.

The author has sometimes entertained the paradox that he would take away the grandest impression of ancient Rome, who should have seen it for the shortest time. He shall have entered by the Porta del Popolo, and then — as usual — be driven to the custom-house, an ancient temple. Then passing under the column of Trajan, in its excavated forum, and by that of Constantine, he shall proceed on, through the great Forum and by the Colosseum, and through the gate of St. John, on his road to Naples; glimpsing the Appian Way, with its tombs, and the long line of ruined aqueducts; proposing to return to Rome and never returning.

It must be understood that exterior ancient Rome is alone here spoken of. Interior ancient Rome is inexhaustible; and produces the greater impression the longer it is studied. And under this head are to be included not only its vast public museums — its Capitol and its Vatican — but its huge private palaces and villas, each in itself a museum. The very gate-posts of these palaces may be the milliaria, by which Horace counted the miles from Rome to Brindisi; while the walls that enclose the villa-grounds will be found brecciated with antique fragments of frieze or cornice. We must include too the almost countless churches, whose innumerable columns have been the columns of ancient fanes; and their tombs, (of prince or pope,) ancient Sarcophagi; whose chapels and shrines are lustrous with the jaspers and chalcedonies of old time; or softly tempered by moon-like alabasters, from far distant Asian or African quarries, long since exhausted or forgotten. — Altogether it may be said that ancient Rome most satisfies, in the same way that its greatest modern temple, St. Peter's, most satisfies; not so much by any one simultaneous general effect, as by degrees, and through an aggregation of particulars.

The first view of St. Peter's has disappointed many a traveller. But as we examine, we are impressed by the details. By its numerous chapels — by its rich altars and shrines — by its many-languaged confessionals, for the penitents of all lands; and by the wide, wide arches that bear up that stupendous dome. Then come

pillars of marble or granite, with their gilded capitals ; and pillars
of solid bronze; and noblest sculptures; and the thoughts of earth's
greatest painters made part of the very walls in calm frescoe; or
to be preserved for ever in imperishable mosaics.   And there is the
great music ; and the deep after-silence ; yet ready to start again
into echo, when some huge portal is suddenly closed.   And then
it has its own equable atmosphere, which in its very equability,
seems to seclude and separate those aisles from the variable world
without ; and which, like the somewhat pensive climate, and the
un-city-like stillness of the city around, disposes to perceive and
to meditate.

Thus (so at least it has seemed to the present writer) in the case
of the ancient city, as of the modern church, it is from accumula-
tion of details, more than from any one general effect, that is
derived the great impression.

Page 30.   Line 16.

The very earth seems odorous of the Past.

Among the notes to Mr. Rogers's " Pleasures of Memory " (notes
as carefully polished as the verses which they accompany) will be
found the following : —

" When a traveller, who was surveying the ruins of Rome, ex-
pressed a desire to possess some relic of its ancient grandeur,
Poussin, who attended him, stooped down ; and gathering up a

handful of earth, shining with small grains of porphyry, "Take this home (said he) for your cabinet and say boldly, ' Questa è Roma antica.' "

In this sense it adds value to the small imitative vases and pillars and other ornaments, which travellers procure at Rome to decorate their northern chimney-pieces, to think that these are, almost all of them, made out of the very marbles, which were the glories of the ancient city. So too the diamonds and the rubies, matters in their nature well nigh indestructible, which now sparkle or glow in the saloons of Paris or of London, may have been as joyfully worn, long ages since, in the palaces of Persia or Egypt, by Esther or by Cleopatra.

Page 34.   Line 9.

This structure near, mere peasant's dwelling-place.

"La route que je parcourais, était bordée de chaque côté par des maisons villageoises. L'architecte a su donner à toutes ces maisons une justesse de proportion et une élégance des formes inconnues dans nos climats. (It is a Swiss who speaks.) Toujours ces maisons sont placées en arrière du chemin, et separées de celui-ci par un mur d'appui et une terrasse de quelques pieds de largeur." — *Lettres d'Italie, par Chateauvieux*, p. 97.

Page 35.   Line 2.

With one full glow of ripest, yellowest maize.

The same writer, speaking of the yet uncut maize, says :—" Ces plantes, rangées dans un ordre parfait, élèvent majestueusement leurs fleurs jaunissantes ; et donnent je ne sais quel air des pompes aux campagnes d'Italie, qui ajoute à leur beauté."

So too, when gathered and hung out, in regular rows, to dry in the sun, the golden heads of this plant decorate and enliven the farm-houses not less.

Page 36.   Line 3.

Its cistern — some antique sarcophagus.

At Tivoli an ancient sarcophagus, or bagnuolo, forms a fountain-cistern.

Page 36.   Line 13.

From forth whose shapely rims dewed vine-leaves drop.

Sculptors have derived the ornamental vine-leaves, which they wind round the rims of their vases, from this every-day fact.   And a distinguished traveller has informed the writer that he has seen vine-leaves habitually preferred for this purpose, even where cork was the common growth of the country.

Page 38. Line 4.

'Tis Homer's simile, so we may dare.

"Βοῶπις Ἥρη·"—*Homer's Iliad.* Pope and Cowper have both evaded the word ; certainly not easy to manage.

Page 38. Line 6.

Now thro' the spacious court behold they go.

Such combinations of rural simplicity and civic grandeur are perpetually presenting themselves in Italy. It was in the fine court yard of the Palazzo Maffei at Verona that the author remembers to have looked, long since (for such impressions do not soon pass away), on the sort of vintage scene which he has here attempted to describe, and characterize.

Page 39. Line 5.

Then that old Crone, with lifted tambourine.

The author had the good fortune to be present in company with Miss Sedgwick and some other friends at a somewhat similar scene — at Baiæ — near Naples. Miss Sedgwick has described the occasion in her very agreeable " Letters from Abroad." The following is part of what she says:— "Our merry followers were joined by an old woman.... She was the living image

of Raphael's Cumæan Sybil . . . the same wrinkled brow, and
channelled cheeks; and unquenched energy burning in her eye;
the resemblance was perfect even to the two protruding teeth. She
was sitting on the fragment of a marble column, holding above her
head a tambourine, on which she was playing one of the wild airs
to which they dance the tarantella, and accompanying it with her
cracked voice. . . . My merry girl danced and shouted like a frantic
Bacchante. I never saw . . . an eye, whose brightness was so near
the wildness of insanity." — *Letters from Abroad*, Moxon, 1st edit.
p. 285.

Page 40.   Line 7.

That cumber, many a league, the valleys round.

" A long track of ruins hangs from the shoulders of the Ross
Berg, a distance of four or five miles.   Its greatest breadth may
be three miles; and the triangular area of the ruins is fully equal
to that of Paris, taken at the external boulevards or about double
the extent of the inhabited city.

" The high road ascends vast hillocks of rubbish, calculated to
be thirty feet deep hereabouts; but near the centre of the valley
probably two hundred feet; and winds among enormous blocks of
stone, already beginning to be moss-grown, and with herbage
springing up between them." — MURRAY's *Swiss Handbook*,
pp. 43, 44.

Page 41.   Line 5.

E'en Jove himself — Great Jove Capitoline.

" In mentioning the curiosities of this church, the statue of St.
Peter should not be omitted, which stands against the last pillar of
the nave, next to the Baldacchino.   A Roman antiquary informs
us that this was made by order of St. Leo out of the bronze of a
statue of Jupiter Capitolinus."— Burton's *Rome*, vol. ii. p. 181.

Page 48.   Line 14.

The green acanthus, as in mockery,
And wild, as when by chance in wicker sown,
It gave, of old, its graceful hint to stone.

Alluding to the asserted origin of the Corinthian capital.

Page 50.   Line 14.

The various plain, from hill to circling sea.

" Before us — the opening valley exhibited a distant perspective,
over the Campagna, to the seven hills and the towers of Rome, and
· the Mediterranean closing, or rather bordering the picture with a
gleam of purple."   So writes Eustace at Tivoli (vol. ii. p. 416.).

R

Page 52.   Line 6.

" Meanings never meant."

The author has marked this as a quotation.   Whether it be such or no he has not been able to learn.

NOTES.

OCCASIONAL VERSES.

Page 91.
THE GREEK WIFE.

This poem was written to illustrate an engraving.

Page 106.   Line 9.

Or gets by hooks and crooks.

The law compels every new publication to deliver itself into the hands of the Keeper of the Books, unpaid for.   And these are the "hooks and crooks" of which authors and publishers are prone occasionally to complain.

Page 107.   Line 5.

Cum tu coëmptos undique nobiles
Libros Panæti.

It is needful to state, as briefly as may be, under what circumstances this happy quotation was made.

At the hospitable and classical table of the Rev. Dr. Williams, the present Warden of New College, one of the guests had assigned, among other motives for a lengthened summer stay in town "the society of friends;" and had mentioned, with names of other friends, that of Mr. Panizzi.—When, (on its being stated, in answer to an inquiry of one of the party that Mr. Panizzi was keeper of the printed books at the British Museum,) out flashed Mr. Erle's aptest quotation, with the pleasant remark that "old Horace had given just the same reason for stopping at Rome."

Page 109.

THE GODS OF GREECE.

This paraphrase has been made through the medium of a literal English translation; the writer himself not knowing German.

Whether successful as a paraphrase, or not, at least it has been glorified as having called forth Miss E. B. Barrett's (now Mrs. Browning's) noble lyric of the "Dead Pan."

Page 116.

" Graceful Palms of Bordighiera,
  Bending o'er the Riviera,

Grove than yours was never fairer —
Graceful palms of Bordighiera."

These four lines were the graceful impromptu of a deceased female friend (whose mind was open to all forms of the Good and the Beautiful) as she passed along the cornice road from Genoa to Nice. They have been extended, as here printed, by the present writer.

Page 129.

This is a slight attempt to translate Anacreon more briefly than is usually done, and it claims no merit beyond its brevity.

Page 141.   Line 5.

The fire-wheeled bark would part.   Storm saith her " Nay."

Since this was written the author's accomplished friend, the Rev. John Eagles, has pointed out to him a somewhat similar passage in Ariosto's Orlando, Canto 2, Stanza 28, 29.

Il vento si sdegnò, &c.

" Non convien', dice il vento, che io comporti
Tanta licenza, che v' avete tolta."

The same learned friend has also indicated some passages very curiously applicable to steam-boats in Homer's description of the ships of the Phæacians. See HOMER's *Odyssey*, 1.554, and on-wards. There are persons who assert, and others who have assented to the assertion, that all the discoveries of the moderns are to be found in the writings of the ancients; for, as good provers can prove — so — good believers — can believe — anything. To such persons these passages will be a " God-send."

Page 164.   Line 6.

Where the built organ, through its thousand flutes.

" Then from one chord of his amazing shell
    Would he fetch out the voice of quires and weight
    Of the built organ."

These lines will be found in Mr. Leigh Hunt's exquisite frag-ment, entitled " Paganini ; " among his Poetical Works, Moxon, 1844.

Page 164.   Last line.

" *From forth his scrannel-pipe of wretched straw.*" — LYCIDAS.

Page 165.   Line 8.

" *And but for Sunday-service cleansed from dust.*"
RHYMED PLEA FOR TOLERANCE.

Page 165.   Line 16.

Could make " a sunshine in the shady place." — SPENSER.

Page 176.   Line 16.

Meets the tides with equal war.

It is said that the voyager " going out to sea and sailing with a good breeze for hours, sees nothing on any side but the white and turbid waters of the Mississippi, long after he is out of sight of land." — *Description of the Mississippi.*

Page 193.   Line 16.

" In the mid-way of this our mortal life." — CARY's *Dante.*

Page 220.   Line 6.

As they tell
Of drowning men.

The author's attention was drawn to this remarkable fact early in his life.   Since then, through personal intercourse and miscellaneous reading, he has more than once come into contact with the same statement, and has sometimes regretted that he has made no notes of the authorities.   But he is aware of two distinguished

living witnesses.   The one, the present Admiral Beaufort, Hydro-
grapher to the Navy, whose statement will be found in the late Sir
John Barrow's Autobiography, p. 398. — The other, the author's
personal friend, Sir Charles Fellows.   He narrowly escaped death
by drowning at Naples — and, at the present writer's request, has
more than once related to him the intensely rapid passage of
thought which he then experienced.

THE END.

LONDON :

SPOTTISWOODES and SHAW,
New-street-Square.

L. H
12/22

RETURN TO ➡ CIRCULATION DEPARTMENT
202 Main Librar

ALL BOOKS MAY BE RECALLED AFTER 7 DAYS
1-month loans may be renewed by calling 642-3405
6-month loans may be recharged by bringing books to Circulation Desk
Renewals and recharges may be made 4 days prior to due date

Lightning Source UK Ltd.
Milton Keynes UK
UKHW01f1846010518

321959UK00031B/673/P